MEET UNITED GERMANY

Handbook 1991/92

Edited by Susan Stern

MEET UNITED GERMANY

Handbook 1991/92

A publication of the
Frankfurter Allgemeine Zeitung GmbH
Information Services
and Atlantik-Brücke e.V.

Die Deutsche Bibliothek – CIP-Einheitsaufnahme

Meet United Germany / a publication of the Frankfurter Allgemeine Zeitung GmbH Information Services and Atlantik-Brücke. Ed. by Susan Stern. - Frankfurt am Main : Frankfurter Allg. Zeitung, 1991
ISBN 3-924875-73-1
NE: Stern, Susan [Hrsg.]; Atlantik-Brücke e.V.

Editor: Susan Stern
Deputy editor: Ilka Eßmüller
Cover illustrator: Walter Hanel
Graphic design: Dietmar Ostermann

Table of Contents

C   Miscellaneous

Addresses. To avoid confusion and distinguish between the western and eastern parts of Germany, we have followed the recommendation of the Deutsche Bundespost (German postal service) and precede postal codes with a "W" or an "O". Thus, W-6000 Frankfurt is the western city Frankfurt/Main, and O-1200 Frankfurt is the eastern city Frankfurt/Oder. The Bundespost claims that the W and the O will speed up mail delivery.

Phone Numbers. We give numbers outside Germany according to the standard pattern: (country code + local code) + individual number. As an example: the German-French Chamber of Commerce in Paris is given as: (33 1) 40 58 35 35.

In most cases, we give numbers within Germany as they would be dialled from western Germany: (inner German code) + individual number. Thus, a Frankfurt/Main number is preceded by (069), a Hamburg number by (040), a Berlin (East) number by (00 37 2), a Dresden number by (00 37 51). To dial these numbers from outside Germany, the initial zero (or zeros as the case may be) must be omitted. As an example: to call Frankfurt/Main from the UK, dial international code 010 + western German code 49 + Frankfurt code 69 + individual number. To call Dresden, dial international code 010 + eastern German code 37 + Dresden code 51 + individual number.

Decimal Dots and Commas. The Anglo-Saxon world views anything less than one as slightly dotty and anything over one thousand as pointless. It therefore uses the decimal point (or dot) system; the number one million three hundred and fifty thousand two hundred and ten and a half is written: 1,350,210.5

In Germany (as in other countries), the dot/comma system is reversed. The above number is written: 1.350.210,5

The editors (and proofreaders) of this book have done their best to ensure that all numbers are in accordance with the Anglo-Saxon convention.

Geography and Population

Germany lies at the heart of Europe and is surrounded by nine countries. Its southern border with Switzerland and Austria is marked by the Alps; to the east, Germany shares a mountainous frontier with Czechoslovakia and is separated from Poland by the Oder and Neisse rivers. Its western neighbours are the Netherlands, Belgium, Luxembourg and France. Jutting northward from the German mainland is the peninsula of Denmark.

Germany covers an area of 137,744 sq miles (357,000 sq km) and is the third largest EC country after France and Spain. The northern region is a low, wide coastal plain along the North and Baltic seas, and forested highlands dominate the central and southern regions. The country is drained by the Danube, Rhine, Elbe, Weser and Oder river systems. The German segment of the Rhine is 865 km long, all of it navigable. On the southeast side of Europe's continental divide or watershed, the Danube flows eastward from its source in the Black Forest, through Germany (647 km) and Austria to the Black Sea. The highest German mountain (2,962 metres) is the Zugspitze, straddling the border with Austria. The Ore Mountains which form part of the border with Czechoslovakia rise to elevations of 1,214 meters. The Baltic Sea island of Rügen covers an area of 926 sq km.

Most of the country has a typical northwest coastal climate, influenced by moist air masses from the Atlantic. The eastern region is sometimes influenced by the continental high pressure centre, making for somewhat colder winters and warmer summers. Prevailing winds are usually from the west. Summers are moderate; winters are typically rainy and bleak, except in the extreme south, where an alpine climate prevails.

With a population of over 79 million, including 4.6 million foreigners, Germany is the most densely populated country in Europe and makes up 23% of the total EC population. Most Germans live in the western *Länder,* along the middle and lower Rhine from Karlsruhe, near the French border, northward through the highly industrialized Ruhr conurbation to the Dutch border. Overall population density is 222 per sq km (30 fewer per sq km than before unification), which breaks down to 251.4 per sq km in western Germany and 150.5 per sq km in eastern Germany. The most sparsely populated *Land* is Mecklenburg-Vorpommern (82 inhabitants per sq km) and the most densely is Nordrhein-Westfalen (502 per sq km). In 1990, the western German birth rate exceeded the death rate for the first time since 1972, which indicates that the country's population may be growing again. However, the birthrate in eastern Germany has decreased since unification.

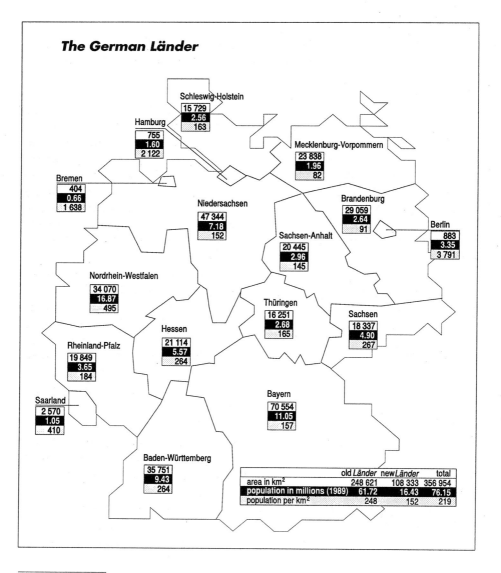

The German Länder

Schleswig-Holstein
15 729 / 2.56 / 163

Hamburg
755 / 1.60 / 2 122

Mecklenburg-Vorpommern
23 838 / 1.96 / 82

Bremen
404 / 0.66 / 1 638

Niedersachsen
47 344 / 7.18 / 152

Brandenburg
29 059 / 2.64 / 91

Berlin
883 / 3.35 / 3 791

Sachsen-Anhalt
20 445 / 2.96 / 145

Nordrhein-Westfalen
34 070 / 16.87 / 495

Thüringen
16 251 / 2.68 / 165

Sachsen
18 337 / 4.90 / 267

Hessen
21 114 / 5.57 / 264

Rheinland-Pfalz
19 849 / 3.65 / 184

Saarland
2 570 / 1.05 / 410

Bayern
70 554 / 11.05 / 157

Baden-Württemberg
35 751 / 9.43 / 264

	old *Länder*	new *Länder*	total
area in km²	248 621	108 333	356 954
population in millions (1989)	61.72	16.43	76.15
population per km²	248	152	219

Structure of the Federal Government

The government consists of three parts: the legislature (the Bundestag and the Bundesrat), the executive (chancellor, cabinet, bureaucracy) and the judiciary.

The Bundestag. The Bundestag (lower house of parliament) is the supreme legislative authority. Its members or deputies are elected for four years by the voting public (German citizens aged 18 and over) in direct, free, equal and secret elections in a procedure which combines the direct election of candidates with proportional representation: half of the deputies are elected directly, the other half through a complex party list system (this to ensure that while the deputies represent the will of the people, they do not represent too many wills of too many people and become, as in times past, too fragmented). Because of the nature of the electoral system, the number of deputies in the Bundestag is not absolutely fixed; in the December 1990 general election (the first general election to be held after unification), 663 voting deputies were returned.

Deputies belong to the various political parties. In order to keep the number of parties down and ensure that parliament and government can function efficiently, only parties which poll at least 5% of the votes or win a minimum of three seats in the direct vote may be represented in the Bundestag. In principle, deputies are not bound by mandates and instructions but are free to vote according to their conscience, and if a deputy can no longer identify with the policies of his party and chooses to leave, he does not lose his Bundestag seat. In practice, however, deputies tend to retain party loyalty (until their conscience or interests are stretched to the limit) and, in line with their party allegiances, form *Fraktionen* (parliamentary groups). The size of these groups determines the composition of the parliamentary committees, and it is in these committees that most legislation is worked out and prepared for presentation; plenary sessions in the Bundestag are reserved for the more important (and controversial) issues of home and foreign policy, as well as for the final stage of the voting on a bill.

In addition to making laws, the Bundestag has a few other responsibilities: it elects the federal chancellor (the designated leader of the strongest party) and keeps the government in check. Thus, minority groups in the Bundestag can

Structure of the Federal Government

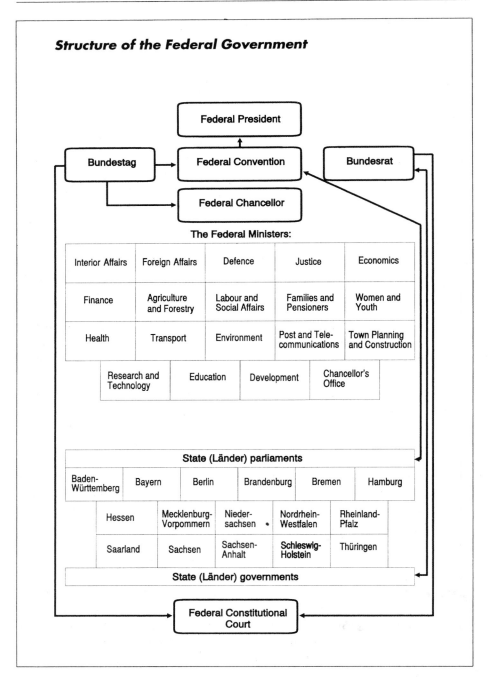

demand information from the government or request the appointment of a committee of enquiry.

The Bundesrat. The Bundesrat (upper house of parliament or federal council) is composed of representatives of the *Länder* (state) governments. The number of appointed representatives a state may have (and thus, the number of votes it commands) is dependent on the size of the state, the smallest sending three representatives, the largest sending five. The votes of each state are cast as a block, and all decisions are made by the government of the state and not by the individual representatives. Since state and national elections do not coincide, the composition of the upper house may change during the lifetime of a particular federal government. Laws may or may not require the approval of the Bundesrat; the proportion is theoretically about 50:50. The laws that need approval are primarily those which affect the states directly, either fiscally or administratively (and as the states claim that more and more laws affect them, they also claim the right of approval in more and more cases). Where Bundesrat approval is not necessary, the upper house has the right to object, although the objection can be overruled by the Bundestag. If Bundestag and Bundesrat are unable to agree, a conference committee composed of members of both houses must be convened and is usually able to reach a compromise. Only in cases where the states are directly responsible for legislation (in matters of education, law and order, etc.) does the Bundesrat actually have the power of veto. Since Bundesrat members represent not just their state, but also the strongest political party of that state, party-political interests play a significant role in Bundesrat decisions. Thus, when there is a difference in party strength in the Bundestag and the Bundesrat, agreement between the two houses may be held up, at least temporarily.

The Bundesregierung. The Bundesregierung (federal government) in Bonn consists of the federal chancellor and his cabinet of federal ministers. The federal chancellor is formally nominated by the federal president and elected by the Bundestag – in fact, each political party announces its chancellor candidate before the election, and the candidate of the winning party becomes the chancellor. The federal ministers are nominated by the chancellor and formally appointed by the federal president. The chancellor has considerable power: he establishes government policy guidelines within which his ministers direct their departments. He and his cabinet can make major policy decisions, but they are accountable to parliament for their actions, and it is possible for the Bundestag to replace the government through a vote of no-confidence against the chancellor (although not against the ministers). There are strong safeguards against the ousting of the government,

The Legislative Process

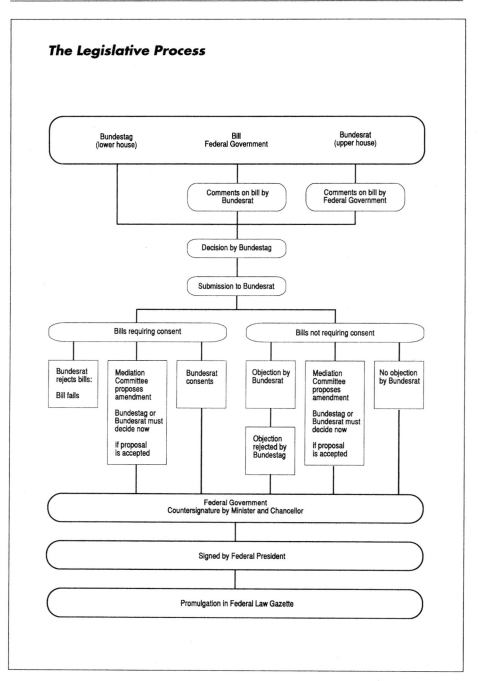

and in the forty-year history of the Federal Republic, although several no-confidence motions have been introduced, only one has succeeded: the 1982 overthrow of Chancellor Helmut Schmidt, who was replaced by Helmut Kohl.

The Bundespräsident. The Bundespräsident (federal president) is the head of state of the Federal Republic of Germany. Elected for five years by the Bundesversammlung (a constitutional body which exists only for that purpose), re-electable only once, the president is to a large extent a figurehead with a number of formal functions but little real authority. Nevertheless, as the representative of the Federal Republic in its relations with other countries, the president performs an important role, and the current incumbent, Richard von Weizsäcker, has done a great deal since 1984 for the good of the country's image.

The Judiciary. Administration of justice in the Federal Republic is divided between the federation and the *Länder*. There are "ordinary" courts for civil and criminal law, as well as special administrative, labour, social and fiscal courts. All of the lower courts are administered by the *Länder*, and only in the final instance does a case come before a federal court.

On the federal level, there are five supreme courts whose responsibility is to ensure a uniform interpretation of the law. At the peak of the judicial structure is the Bundesverfassungsgericht (federal constitutional court). An institution introduced with the creation of the Federal Republic, its primary purpose is to protect the Basic Law and make sure that all legislation is compatible with it – hence its nickname, "guardian of the constitution". Half of the federal judges of the Bundesverfassungsgericht are elected by the Bundestag, the other half by the Bundesrat; judges serve for twelve years and cannot be re-elected. They preside over two senates, one dealing with individual rights, the other with political conflicts.

The German Länder (States)

The Five New Eastern Länder

The eastern *Länder* are "new" in two respects: they joined the 11 "old" *Länder* of the Federal Republic in 1990, at which time they were newly reinstated. In 1952, the East German communist regime had replaced them by 14 *Bezirke* (administrative regions which were simply local organs of state power). Since they had not been dissolved by official constitutional amendment, after the collapse of the regime they could simply revert to their original status.

Brandenburg. Brandenburg, with a land area of 29,059 sq km, is the largest of the new eastern Länder. It occupies a portion of the North German Plain east of the Elbe and west of the Oder rivers. The *Land* shares a long frontier with Poland along the Oder River and also surrounds the independent city-state of Berlin. Brandenburg has only 2,641,152 inhabitants and among the five new eastern *Länder* ranks next to last in population density (91 people per sq km). Second in the region in agricultural output despite generally poor soil, it is next to last in regional industrial production.

The only eastern *Land* to give a plurality to the Social Democrats in the October 1990 state elections, Brandenburg is governed by a coalition led by Social Democratic Premier Manfred Stolpe. Junior partners in his government include liberal Free Democrats and the environmentalist Alliance 90.

Fruit, vegetables, potatoes, sugar beets and grains are the main produce of Brandenburg, with Berlin providing an ideal market. Pigs are raised on large collective farms that are only slowly being privatized.

Brandenburg also has heavy machinery, cement and vehicle manufacturing industries and manufactures china and ceramics, thanks to its deposits of limestone and fine clays. Lignite is mined and petroleum refined. Some electrical manufacturing is located around Berlin.

The capital city of Potsdam (pop. 141,430) was once a residence of Prussian rulers. Located southwest of Berlin, it served as the site of the postwar allied conference that divided Germany. Other large centres include Cottbus (pop.

128,943), Frankfurt on the Oder (pop. 87,126), Brandenburg (pop. 93,441) and Eisenhüttenstadt (pop. 52,393). An ethnic minority of about 60,000 Slavic Sorbs lives in the rural Niederlausitz district on the southern border with Sachsen.

Mecklenburg-Vorpommern (Mecklenburg-Western Pomerania). Predominantly agricultural, Mecklenburg-Vorpommern stretches along the Baltic coastal plain from Schleswig-Holstein in the west to Poland in the east. It is a flat region with 600 lakes and numerous peninsulas and sea islands along the broken coastline. The *Land* has an area of 23,838 sq km. It is the most sparsely populated of the new eastern *Länder* with a total population of 1,963,909 and a population density of 82 people per sq km.

Since the 14 October 1990 state elections, the Christian Democrats have governed in coalition with the Free Democrats. But the coalition, led by Premier Alfred Gomulka, has only a slender voting edge over the opposition Social Democrats and Democratic Socialists (PDS).

The baroque capital city of Schwerin (pop. 129,492) was founded by the Guelf King Henry the Lion in 1160 and later was home to the dukes of Mecklenburg. The Baltic seaport Rostock (pop. 252,956) is the state's largest city. Other important towns are the agricultural market centre of Neubrandenburg (pop. 90,953) and the university town of Greifswald (pop. 68,270).

Farming, fishing and food processing dominate the economy in the absence of significant mining or manufacturing. The seaports of Rostock, Stralsund, Wismar and Wolgast are hard pressed by the competitive problems of the regional shipbuilding industry and the loss of their vital Comecon trade with Eastern European ports. The *Land* hopes to balance its economy through a build-up of tourism at its traditional coastal resorts and the Baltic islands, such as Rügen.

Sachsen (Saxony). Sachsen, with an area of 18,337 sq km, is a wide, urbanized and industrial corridor stretching along the rugged Czech border of eastern Germany from Poland on the northeast to Bayern on the southwest. The relatively crowded *Land* is home to over 4.9 million people. It leads eastern Germany in industrial production and in population density with 267 people per sq km.

Christian Democrats led by Kurt Biedenkopf swept to an absolute majority in the October 1990 state parliamentary elections.

Once an independent kingdom, Sachsen has been known through the centuries for its talented craftsmen and shrewd entrepreneurs. Its 18th century monarch was also the king of Poland.

The capital of Sachsen is Dresden (see Dresden, pages 43-44). Leipzig, (pop. 530,000) is known for its semi-annual trade fairs and for the 1812 Battle of the Nations in which Napoleon was defeated by a superior allied force (see Leipzig, pages 53-54). Chemnitz (pop. 301,918) was known as Karl Marx Stadt under the communist regime; forming an industrial triangle with Dresden and Leipzig, it is an important textile centre. Near the Czech border, Klingenthal manufactures toys and musical instruments. Trabant automobiles were made at Zwickau (pop. 118,914), motorcycles at Zschopau and rolling stock at Görlitz (pop. 74,766) and Zittau (pop. 36,246).

The transition from a command to a market economy has hit Sachsen hard. The manufacture of Trabants will be discontinued, although Volkswagen is planning major investment in the region. Dresden's Pentacon camera company was the first big casualty of unification, but limited camera production may be revived in 1993 with western investment. Parts of the Sachsen landscape have been marred by the strip mining of lignite, now no longer in demand. But western German and foreign banks have taken an interest in Dresden and industrial companies are setting up base there.

Sachsen-Anhalt (Saxony-Anhalt). Sachsen-Anhalt ranks third among the five new eastern *Länder* in size and population density as well as in agricultural and industrial production. From its borders with Brandenburg and Mecklenburg in the Elbe River basin, its 20,445 sq km sprawl southwestward to meet Niedersachsen in the west and Thüringen and Sachsen in the south. The *Land* has a population of 2,964,971.

Since the October 1990 elections, Sachsen-Anhalt has been governed by a coalition of Christian Democrats and Free Democrats under Christian Democrat Gerd Gies. (Update: as of July 1991, under Werner Münch.)

The capital of Magdeburg, a city of 288,355 on the Elbe, serves the agricultural north as a market centre. Some of Germany's richest agricultural land is in this region. The mining of lignite, gypsum and potash and their use in associated chemical industries have created massive pollution problems in the industrial southern area bordering Sachsen and Thüringen. Loss of Comecon markets for these industries and a reorientation toward western German environmental standards and energy supplies confront Sachsen-Anhalt with major structural problems. The chemical giant Leuna-Werk has been closing down antiquated production facilities in the region.

Halle (pop. 230,000), Sachsen-Anhalt's second largest city, is an industrial centre on the Saale River. Other important centres include Bitterfeld (pop. 20,017), which won the dubious distinction as Europe's most polluted city, and Zeitz (pop. 44,000). The state's copper deposits have been depleted or are only marginally economical.

Thüringen (Thuringia). Thüringen ranks second in population among the eastern German *Länder* with 2,693,877 inhabitants, averaging 165 to the sq km. It is also the smallest *Land* in the region, with an area of 16,251 sq km. Thüringen borders on Hessen, Niedersachsen and Bayern to the west and south and on Sachsen and Sachsen-Anhalt to the east and north. It is eastern Germany's second most important industrial region after Sachsen.

State Premier Josef Duchac led the Christian Democrats to victory in the October 1990 state elections.

The *Land* capital of Erfurt (pop. 217,035) is centrally located. The nearby city of Weimar (pop. 61,583) gave its name to the ill-fated German democracy that existed between the world wars. Jena (pop. 105,825) is the main base of the eastern half of the giant Zeiss optics concern. Precision instruments, optics and engineering are also key industries in Gera (pop. 132,257), Eisfeld and Saalfeld. Eisenach (pop. 47,027) was the home of Wartburg automobile manufacturing (discontinued), and now provides a base for an Opel subsidiary of General Motors. Potassium is mined in the Werra River and Harz Mountain region and uranium is mined in the east.

The agricultural sector is relatively small, but Thuringian soil is regarded as good. An abundance of mountains and forests should also give Thüringen a head start in developing its tourism industry.

Berlin. The reconstituted city-state of Berlin now embraces what had been divided into East Berlin and West Berlin (see Berlin, pages 36-38).

The Ten Western Länder

The region that was formerly West Germany boasts Europe's strongest economy. The value of production in this region of Germany is roughly a third greater than that of France, the closest European contender. It is around half the size of the Japanese economy and a quarter the size of the US economy.

The region's labour pool approaches 30 million, including more than 2 million foreigners. Thanks to unification and the opening up of Eastern Europe, in 1990 the economy of western Germany turned in its most dynamic performance since 1974. With most industries operating at full capacity for a second straight year, business investment was up 13%. The economy expanded by a real 4.6% after 3.9% in 1989 and 3.6% in 1988. Nominal GNP for the region, including West Berlin, came to DM 2,447.7 million while inflation remained under 3%, thanks partly to the appreciation of the currency.

Nordrhein-Westfalen (North Rhine-Westphalia). Germany's most industrialized and most populous *Land* with around 16.7 million residents, Nordrhein-
Westfalen sprawls eastward from the Dutch and Belgian borders over an area of
34,068 sq km. To the east and north, Nordrhein-Westfalen borders on Niedersachsen, to the south and southeast on Rheinland-Pfalz and Hessen. The Rhine River
flows northwestward through the centre of the state, which, despite its high
population density of 489 per sq km, still has room for horse breeding, cattle and
pig raising and the cultivation of sugar beet, wheat and barley.

Eleven of the 20 largest West German cities in the 1986 census were in
Nordrhein-Westfalen, which contains the densely settled industrial heartland of
Germany: the Ruhr district, where the mining of rich deposits of bituminous coal
spawned a vast iron and steel industry in the 19th century. Today, key industries
in Nordrhein-Westfalen include electronics, chemicals, machinery and plant engineering, automotive engineering, synthetic fibres, paints, aluminium smelting,
brewing, cement, glass and textiles.

The seat of the *Land* government is Düsseldorf (pop. 562,000), which is
also a wealthy centre of finance and fashion (see Düsseldorf, pages 44-46). Bonn
(pop. 291,000), the present seat of the federal government (see Bonn, pages 38-39)
is in the far southeast corner of the *Land*. Other major cities, their names closely
linked to the steel, chemical, petroleum and engineering industries, include
Cologne (pop. 916,000; see Cologne, pages 41-42), Essen (pop. 620,000; see Essen,
pages 46-47), Dortmund (pop. 572,000), Duisburg (pop. 518,000), Wuppertal
(pop. 377,000), Bochum (pop. 382,000), Bielefeld (pop. 300,000) and Gelsenkir-
chen (pop. 285,000).

A disproportionately high number of Germany's top 100 industrial companies are based in Nordrhein-Westfalen. The list includes Thyssen, Bayer, Krupp,
Hoesch, RWE, Mannesmann, Klöckner-Humboldt-Deutz and Deutsche Babcock.
Around a third of western Germany's exports and some 26% of its gross domestic
product are produced in this *Land*. Although this concentration was once even
greater, no other *Land* even comes close to these levels. The global steel depres-
sion that lasted from the mid-Seventies to the mid-Eighties and the growth of the
electronics, finance and service industries in southern Germany triggered well-
justified fears of economic decline for this region of heavy industry. The gloomy
predictions were premature. Nordrhein-Westfalen sprang back to economic vita-
lity in the late Eighties with the recovery of the steel industry and a general upswing
in global trade and foreign demand for German capital goods. The jobless rate,
which was in double digits in the mid-Eighties, has fallen again to the national
average, currently just under 7%. Business investment has soared and the *Land*
has been attracting close to a quarter of all foreign direct investment in Germany.

Nordrhein-Westfalen has been steadily courting Japanese investment and Düsseldorf (see Düsseldorf, pages 44-46) is said to have the largest Japanese community outside Nippon. Düsseldorf, Cologne and Essen are the sites of some of Germany's major trade fairs. The Ruhr is no longer a grimy monoculture of smoke-stack industries. Blighted industrial areas have been modernized, developed for new uses or turned into leafy park and recreational tracts. Service industries have taken root in the large centres, which boast a rich assortment of cultural attractions.

Bayern (Bavaria). Once an independent kingdom allied with Austria, Bayern is geographically the largest of all the German *Länder:* over 70,553 sq km, from its Alpine frontier with Austria in the south to the border of Hessen and Thüringen in the north, and from Czech Bohemia on the east to Baden-Württemberg in the west. Roughly the size of Scotland, its population is only 11 million, averaging 156 people to the sq km. Predominantly agricultural until World War II, Bayern has industrialized rapidly in the past few decades. It now generates 18% of Germany's gross domestic product, putting it second to Nordrhein-Westfalen. Bayern's strategy has concentrated on advanced technologies and its growing electrical engineering industry turned over DM 49 billion in 1989. The industry employed 260,000 in 1990, mostly in the Munich and Nuremberg areas. Around 43% of the electrical products made in Bayern are sold abroad, the European Community accounting for 55%. Electrical giant Siemens, Germany's second largest company, is headquartered in the Bavarian capital of Munich, where numerous young computer hard- and software firms have put down roots (see Munich, pages 54-56).

Bayern also has its core of military contractors, including tank manufacturer Krauss-Maffei, Daimler-Benz aerospace subsidiary Messerschmidt-Bölkow-Blohm (MBB) and Daimler aircraft turbine maker Maschinen- und Turbinen Union (MTU) at Munich. FAG Kugelfischer makes ball bearings at Schweinfurt. In the automotive branch, BMW makes luxury cars and MAN turns out heavy trucks and vehicles in Munich, while Audi sedans are produced at Ingolstadt, a city also noted for its refineries and petrochemical plants. Deckel and Maho are in mechanical engineering, the second largest industrial sector in Bayern, centred around Augsburg and Nuremberg. Sportsware companies Adidas and Puma engage in intra-family rivalry in Franconia. Quelle, one of Europe's biggest mail-order houses, is headquartered near Nuremberg.

Breweries are also important in beer-drinking Bayern, where most of Germany's hops are grown in the low-lying region south of the Danube. Bayern produces a quarter of western Germany's crops and a third of its timber. Family farms predominate. Between the Main and the Danube rivers lies the heavily agricultural region of Franconia.

Nuremberg (pop. 465,000), the Franconian capital, is the centre of toy manufacturing. Augsburg (pop. 245,000) is Bayern's third largest city. The Rhine-Main-Danube Canal being dug through Bayern is scheduled to open in 1993, completing an inland water route between the Black Sea and the North Sea. Politically, Bayern is a conservative state, firmly in the hands of the Christian Social Union, the Bavarian wing of the Christian Democrats, for most of the past three decades. In big cities such as Munich, however, the Social Democrats are strong contenders.

Hessen (Hesse). Hessen stretches from the heavily populated region at the confluence of the Rhine and Main rivers in the southwest to the valley of the Weser, Fulda and Werra rivers in the northeast. While Hessen covers only 21,114 sq km, it ranks fourth in production in western Germany, generating around 10% of the region's gross domestic product. Most of the *Land's* 5.5 million people, some 9% of the western German total, live in the Rhine-Main region, which includes the large cities of Frankfurt, Wiesbaden and Darmstadt. Kassel (pop. 184,000), a centre for refining, machinery and automotive engineering, is the leading city in the *Land's* rugged northeast. Centrally located are the industrial towns of Giessen and Wetzlar, a centre of the optics industry, and the university town of Marburg. About a third of Hessen is forested, making it the greenest of the western German *Länder.*

The Wetterau region north of Frankfurt and the Rhine flood plain near Darmstadt are very fertile and ideal for cereals, potatoes, asparagus and sugar beets. High quality white wine is produced in the Rhine valley.

Thanks in large part to Frankfurt's role as Germany's foremost financial centre, prosperous Hessen has been attracting nearly a quarter of all direct foreign investment in western Germany – more than any other *Land* (see Frankfurt, pages 47-49). Close to Frankfurt, Offenbach is a centre of the leather industry. Other Hessian industries include optics, mechanical and electrical engineering and equipment, refining and tyres. Darmstadt hosts Merck and Wella. Giessen has Buderus. Leica is at Wetzlar; Wintershall, Ford and Henschel around Kassel. The Linde machinery group is centred at Wiesbaden, a fashionable and prosperous city of 267,000 and the capital of Hessen. Politically, Hessen has been a Social Democratic stronghold for most of the postwar period. In the Eighties, Christian Democrats began to challenge Social Democrats for control, taking over the state government in a close election in 1987. Four years later, in an equally close election, the Social Democrats returned to power.

The *Land* and the city of Frankfurt are lobbying hard to become the base of the proposed European central bank.

Niedersachsen (Lower Saxony). Second in land area among all the German *Länder*, mostly agrarian Niedersachsen has about 12% of western Germany's population with 7.2 million people, but accounts for only around 9% of the region's gross domestic product. The *Land* covers an area of 47,438 sq km, stretching from the North Sea coast and the Dutch frontier in the west to Sachsen-Anhalt and Mecklenburg in the east. The city-state of Bremen (see Bremen, pages 39-41) is entirely surrounded by Niedersachsen.

Hameln, a town in the *Land's* eastern Brunswick region, was the setting for the medieval tale of the Pied Piper. The capital city of Hanover (pop. 508,000; see Hanover, pages 51-53) along with Celle to the north and Clausthal-Zellerfeld to the south are centres for the regionally significant extraction industries. Continental tyre company and raw materials company Preussag are headquartered at Hanover, which also hosts the world's most important capital goods industrial fair each spring as well as the electronics fair CeBIT. Steel is made at nearby Salzgitter. Just to the east is Wolfsburg, the home base of giant Volkswagen, the *Land's* largest single employer. Göttingen in the southeast is a university town.

Agriculture is king throughout the rest of the *Land*. Niedersachsen leads Germany in the production of pork, poultry, eggs and sugar beet. Part of the German deep-sea fishing fleet is based at Cuxhaven. The Frisian island resorts do a booming tourist trade.

The extraction industries are based on deposits of iron ore, slate, potash, lead, zinc and copper as well as natural gas and some oil. Chemical plants, refining and metalworking have developed around these.

Baden-Württemberg. Baden-Württemberg, the product of the postwar fusion of three small provinces, forms the southwest corner of Germany. The Rhine River divides it from French Alsace and from the German Rhine Palatinate to the west. Switzerland and Lake Constance border on the south side.

The *Land's* area of 37,751 sq km makes it third in size in western Germany. It is home to 9.3 million people, spread 260 to the sq km, and ranks third in western Germany in industrial output, generating 16% of total gross domestic product. Only a century ago, this southwestern region was considered the poorhouse of Germany. Industrialization came rapidly after World War II so that its standard of living has risen above the country's average.

The *Land* is home to Daimler-Benz, now Germany's largest industrial company. It builds its Mercedes cars and trucks at Stuttgart, the centrally located *Land* capital with a population of around 600,000 (see Stuttgart, pages 56-57). Other major industrial centres include Mannheim, Karlsruhe, Heilbronn, Ulm and Pforzheim. The German unit of Swiss-Swedish engineering group ABB is at

Mannheim. Karlsruhe is home to the German atomic research centre as well as to the federal constitutional court.

In addition to automotive engineering, key industries include electronics, optics, chemicals and precision mechanics. And the *Land* is studded with prosperous, family owned machinery manufacturers, a tribute to the ingenuity of the locals. These small machine makers tend to be highly specialized in aspects of automotive equipment, textile manufacturing, electrical supply and machine tools. Baden-Württemberg produces a quarter of the machinery made in western Germany. Baden-Baden, with its gambling casino, as well as the surrounding Black Forest region are popular summer and winter resorts as is the shoreline of the Bodensee (Lake Constance). Agriculture is important in the fertile Rhine plain and eastern terrace lands where cattle are raised and cereals, fruits, vegetables and tobacco are grown. The Black Forest is known for its cherry orchards and cherry brandy as well as for its cuckoo clocks.

Rheinland-Pfalz (Rhineland-Palatinate). Rheinland-Pfalz is centrally located in the western corner of western Germany. The *Land* covers a mostly mountainous area of 19,848 sq km and has a population of 3.6 million, sparsely scattered 182 to the sq km.

Trier, on the Luxembourg border, was an imperial Roman garrison two millennia ago and still boasts its ancient Porta Nigra. Centrally located Kaiserslautern, which makes beer and Pfaff sewing machines, was once a court of the Emperor Barbarossa. The capital city of Mainz (pop. 186,000) was where Johannes Gutenberg invented moveable type. Now it is a university town with a strong printing industry. Industrial Ludwigshafen (pop. 153,000) is the main base of BASF, the international chemical giant. Nearly half of western Germany's shoe industry is centred at Pirmasens. Jewellery is fashioned at Idar-Oberstein. Mechanical engineering is important in Kaiserslautern, Frankenthal and Mainz.

White wine is produced in the valleys of the Rhine, Moselle, Nahe, Saar, Ruwer and Ahr rivers; the *Land* produces two-thirds of Germany's wine. Pumice is quarried in the volcanic Eifel and Hunsrück uplands.

Saarland. The Saarland, with Rheinland-Pfalz to the north and east and French Lorraine to the south and west, is one of Europe's oldest industrial regions as a result of its deposits of coal and iron ore. France and Germany have fought over the industrial Saar and Ruhr, just as they have over Alsace and Lorraine. It was seized by France after World War I but its people voted in a 1935 plebiscite to return to Germany. The same happened after World War II, with the Saarland reverting to German control in 1957. With 2,569 sq km, the *Land* is almost identical in size to Luxembourg, with which it also shares a very short border. It is heavily industrialized and densely populated, with 460 residents to the sq km.

The dominant industry for much of the century was coal and steel. The steel crisis that began in the mid-Seventies forced the *Land* government to virtually take over the Saar operations of Arbed, the Belgian-Luxembourg steel group. The *Land*, which has been controlled by the Social Democrats since the mid-Eighties, has made a determined effort to lure corporate investors from abroad.

Saarbrücken, the capital city, has a population of 186,000.

Schleswig-Holstein. Schleswig-Holstein connects the Danish peninsula to the German mainland. It is washed by the North Sea on the west and the Baltic Sea on the northeast. Terrain ranges from coastal marshes and islands to sandy plains and lake country with low hills. There are popular resorts on the North Frisian islands in the North Sea. The isolated island of Helgoland, further out at sea, also belongs to Schleswig-Holstein, which covers a total area of 15,727 sq km. Its 2.6 million people are thinly distributed and average 166 to the sq km.

The biggest cities are the capital Kiel (pop. 246,000) and Lübeck (pop. 210,000). Flensburg on the Danish border is the home of the German vehicle registration bureau. Both Kiel and the old Hanseatic city of Lübeck are ports on the Baltic. Kiel is also a naval base and a university town with a shipbuilding industry and Germany's only duty free port on the Baltic Sea. The Kiel Canal links the Baltic port with the Elbe estuary and the North Sea. The *Land* lies on the main trade route by land and sea between Scandinavia and the European mainland.

Agriculture, including fishing, is the *Land's* biggest business and features cattle and pig raising and the cultivation of wheat, sugar beet, fruits and vegetables. Holstein farms supply Hamburg with dairy products and other produce. The Baltic and North Sea fringes support a thriving tourist industry.

In centuries past, Germans and Danes fought repeatedly over Schleswig-Holstein. Today, about 30,000 ethnic Danes live in German Schleswig and about twice that many ethnic Germans live in Danish Schleswig. Social Democrats ousted Christian Democrats from the *Land* government in 1988 for the first time in 38 years.

Hamburg. The city-state of Hamburg lies at the head of the Elbe estuary (see Hamburg, pages 49-51).

Bremen. The city-state of Bremen is composed of the port cities of Bremen and Bremerhaven, 60 km apart on the Lower Weser River (see Bremen, pages 39-41).

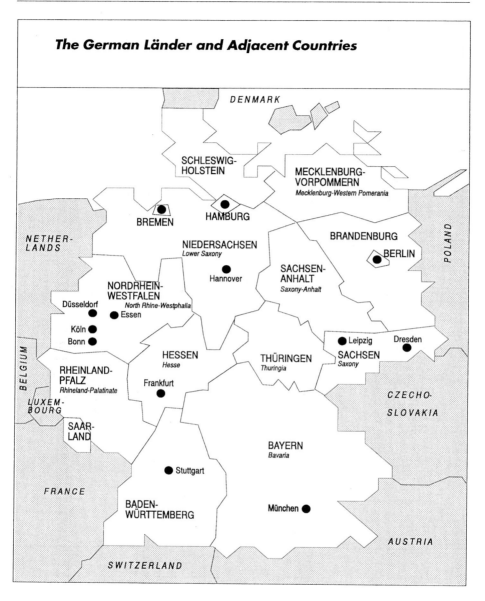

The German Länder and Adjacent Countries

German Cities

It still comes as a surprise to a lot of well-travelled visitors to Germany that there is still no one single "number one" city to match Paris, London, Tokyo or New York. There are quite a few major cities, albeit only four with a population of over a million: Berlin, which now that East and West have joined, boasts 3.4 million, followed at a distance by Hamburg at 1.6 million, Munich at 1.3 million and Cologne just making the grade. Berlin, the once and once-again capital of Germany, is nourishing hopes of out-shadowing all its German rivals and while its chances are good, especially now that it has won its battle to get back the seat of government from Bonn (see Berlin, pages 36-38), for the time being it is not the undisputed hub.

If Berlin, Hamburg, Munich and Cologne are all "large" cities, those with populations between 500,000 and 700,000 are good medium-sized, and there are quite a few qualifiers: Essen, Frankfurt/Main, Hanover, Düsseldorf and Dortmund lead the field with over 600,000 souls, with Leipzig*, Dresden*, Stuttgart, Bremen and Duisburg not far behind (asterisked cities are in eastern Germany). In the next class down, smallish cities (300,000 to 500,000 inhabitants) include Chemnitz*, Halle*, Bochum, Augsburg, Nuremberg, and large towns with less than 300,000 inhabitants include Magdeburg*, Rostock*, Erfurt*, Brunswick, Münster and, of course, the city which for over forty years was the seat of the German government, Bonn (286,000 inhabitants).

The history of Germany explains the present multiplicity of urban centres. The German Empire of the Middle Ages kept expanding and shrinking as different parts of it were won and lost, and by the time the Empire had become the Holy Roman Empire of German States, it was, in fact, no more than a loose conglomeration of separate feudal entities. The German Confederation (Bund) which was founded in 1815 was made up of 41 states, with 37 ruling princes and four free cities, and in 1871 was replaced by a new German Empire, proclaimed as a federal state. Thus, despite all of the vicissitudes, throughout the centuries Germany has remained a collection of more or less sovereign entities, each with its own, well-developed culture and centre, and very often with a strong sense of rivalry.

The provincial capitals of old may have lost their princely patrons and become industrialized, but they retain much of their intellectual heritage and take fierce pride in their cultural life, in their status in the business world (as witness the number of trade fairs) and in their overall attractiveness. That Bonn, an otherwise insignificant small town, became the political centre of the West German federation has to do with the division of Germany after the Second World War and Adenauer's personal insistence; nevertheless, with Berlin out of the running at the time, one of the other much larger and historically more important cities could have been chosen as the new (temporary) capital. Bonn was a diplomatic choice in more ways than one.

Each old German city, with its individual background and traditions, tries to emphasize its uniqueness, to preserve its local identity in the face of the all-pervasive, ever growing commercial and industrial uniformity. While local profile was not uppermost in the minds of town-planners and architects in the West German postwar building boom of the Fifties which resulted in a nightmarish proliferation of ugly boxes from one end of Germany to the other, the tendency now is to restore as many old buildings as possible. The price of modernized, renovated old villas and apartments has been skyrocketing for many years, especially in the major cities (see Property Report, pages 121-130). In some cities, historical sections that were completely or almost completely destroyed during the war have been rebuilt from scratch exactly as they were (part of the Römerberg or City Hall Square in Frankfurt, for example, and the Zwinger complex in Dresden). Modern architecture in western German cities has made a concerted and in many cases successful effort in recent years to blend in with the character of the city, resulting in impressive marriages and at times startling contrasts between the old and the new (as witness the cathedral, main railway station and museum area in central Cologne). Office blocks of the international type found everywhere from Hong Kong to Los Angeles dot the urban German scene too, but they tend to be wealthy and well-maintained, so they are not as offensive as they were a few decades ago. And urban renewal in terms of pedestrian zones and the greening of cities with trees and plants has spread with surprising speed since the Seventies; large and small communities alike have their car-free areas. Unfortunately, these generally lack individual character; almost all of the shops lining the streets belong to national chains, and the cafés, Italian ice cream parlours and fast food stalls all look much the same. After shop closing hours, most pedestrian zones empty almost immediately. Only if they happen to be in the Altstadt (old town) area is there much chance that there will be any kind of street life in the evening; then, they may be surrounded by narrow, winding lanes with "old world atmosphere" and a lot of *Kneipen* (pubs or taverns).

Unification has added a new dimension to urban renewal in Germany. The eastern German cities that have been brought back into the fold are alas! neither what they were before the war, nor interesting "new" cities. What devastation was not caused by Allied bombing was systematically completed and complemented by the socialist regime. Although theoretically a number of buildings in historical city centres were classified as national monuments, the regime did next to nothing to preserve them (except in a few cases in "tourist" cities such as Berlin and Dresden where they were used to attract hard currency) and in the intervening forty years they have fallen into a state of disrepair which may not be reversible. Many old buildings which were considered symbols of decadence, some in relatively good repair after the war, others in need of restoration, were razed to the ground to make way for the symbols of the revolution: the ugliest concrete blocks imaginable. Along the Elbe, for example, these buildings were constructed with their windows facing away from the river – to prevent the inhabitants from being distracted by pleasant scenery from thoughts of a higher order. Air pollution caused by hideous factories spewing out smoky poison (and, of course, by the infamous Trabi car exhausts) has covered most of eastern Germany with a layer of black soot. This has become so ingrained that the very few restorations undertaken by the old regime – the cathedral and the Semper Opera House in Dresden, for instance – look dirty enough to be authentically old (the rebuilding of the opera was completed in 1985).

What lies ahead is the daunting task of recreating and restoring the eastern German cities. It is generally agreed that architectural anarchy should be avoided at all costs, that the cities should be built and rebuilt according to pre-planned careful design. Such designs already exist: architects from all over the world are vying with each other to produce magnificent blueprints. However, there is as yet no money to realize any of the plans. And should investment pour in, there will be property rights questions to be settled, bureaucratic red tape to overcome. Daimler-Benz has prepared a public transportation concept for Berlin, but is not optimistic that their plan (or any other plan) will ever win official approval. The problems are immense – but likewise the challenge.

Not unexpectedly (why should Germany be different from anywhere else?), the cities west and east are not free from crime and prostitution. The "red light" areas are usually centred around the main railway station (but not always: the (in)famous St. Pauli district in Hamburg lies to the west of the city). At the present time, "punk" crime and hooliganism are on the rise in eastern German cities, as unemployment increases and other transition problems disorient the population. Drug trafficking is a serious urban problem (again, often centred around the main railway station), and has contributed to a sharp increase in robberies and more violent crimes. Indiscriminate muggings are all too frequent, and even men are advised not to walk through dark areas or parks at night.

On the subject of parks – many cities have at least one large park in or very close to the centre of town, and some have a surprising number (given the exorbitant price of real estate) of smaller parks. Used throughout the year to exercise small children and dogs, in the summer the parks are dotted with sun-worshipping bodies (these days, often topless or naked) side by side, at least at lunch time, with conservatively dressed businesspeople snatching a few minutes rest to munch a sandwich on a park bench. One unpleasant feature of German cities is the messiness of the pavements. There are no laws in the Federal Republic requiring dog owners to clear up after their pets – or even pull them to the kerb. Most Germans walk with their eyes to the ground and foreign visitors are well advised do the same.

Getting Around in Cities

Public Transportation. Public transportation in western German cities is very good, particularly for the initiated. The system is complex and in many cities involves a network of underground trains (the *S-Bahn* and *U-Bahn*), streetcars or trams (which are becoming rarer these days as the tracks are being laid underground) and buses; ticket-buying and ticket-validation procedures differ from one city to another and there is often a bewildering range of fares. The first-time visitor who has little knowledge of German and is unfamiliar with the different possibilities and combinations is advised to check distances (in some towns, they may be very short) and then decide whether to walk or take a taxi. During trade fairs when taxis can be hard to find, there are often special buses to convey visitors to and fro (information can be obtained from the trade fair centres, tourist offices or hotels and from kiosks at main stations); depending on the city and the fair, there may even be a public address system at the main railway station announcing (in English) how to get to the fair grounds.

Of all the eastern German cities at the present time, only Berlin has a subway system. Most eastern cities, however, have plentiful (if somewhat decrepit) buses and trams which travel at regular intervals.

Taxis. Taxis all over Germany are easy to identify: they are usually beige or white Mercedes, or occasionally Ford Sierras or Opel saloons. They are clearly marked with an overhead taxi sign. Taxi ranks are plentiful although taxis themselves are hard to get during fairs and exhibitions. At most other times, a phone reservation will reliably bring a taxi to the door within 15 minutes (see under individual city for telephone numbers). It is seldom possible to hail a taxi from the street. Eastern Germany has seen considerable entrepreneurship in the taxi business of late, so taxis in the new *Länder* are in good supply.

The Private Car. City driving is seldom a pleasure anywhere, and inside German cities tends to be nerve-wracking. Streets are crowded and off-peak hours are shrinking. Most cities are a maze of one-way streets (which may change from one direction to the other overnight); road-works are the rule and signposts often misleading. The biggest problem, however, is finding a place to park, and the situation is so bad that even illegal parking spaces are difficult or impossible to find. Cities are dotted with multi-storey parking garages which are frequently full, and queuing up to get in can be a long process. Visitors who arrive in a city by car are advised to park it at the hotel and use other forms of transportation (see above).

Walking. Often the quickest way to get around. Visitors are reminded to watch where they tread or to wipe their shoes carefully before entering a building (see page 32).

Hotels

For better or worse, top-class hotels in western Germany are owned, run or are rapidly being taken over by the giant hotel corporations, home-grown and foreign. Each city has an assortment of these international-character establishments in addition to the privately run, usually smaller and more modest places. The Hiltons, Inter-Continentals, Ramadas, Sheratons, Hyatts, Holiday Inns, Queens Moat Houses and Novotels usually identify themselves in the name of the hotel (Frankfurt Inter-Continental, Ramada Parkhotel Munich); very often, the Steigenbergers, Kempinskis, Mövenpicks, Pullman Internationals, Trusthouse Fortes, Best Westerns and Quality Inns (to name but a few) do not, since many of the hotels with a tradition and reputation retain the name they had before being acquired by a chain.

Almost all non-family run hotels can be booked through one or more international reservation services throughout the world, either directly (often through a local charge number) or through a travel agency. Chain-owned hotels in West Germany offer much the same as they do everywhere else: predictable quality and service, reliability and uniformity. It is possible to find a combination of luxury and a degree of individuality (from hotels affiliated with the organization Leading Hotels of the World, for example) but the choice is more limited and comes at a high price. For those looking for a hotel which might, from the inside or outside, give some clue as to the country it happens to be in, it is a good idea to choose a refurbished old establishment with a local (non-chain) name. A hotel with "Hof" in its name (the Frankfurter Hof in Frankfurt, the Bayrischer Hof in Munich, the Breidenbacher Hof in Düsseldorf) was originally built around a courtyard intended for travellers to park their carriages in; although today's visitor is likely to have to park in an underground rabbit warren, the more expensive "Hof" hotels do have a certain atmosphere, if not exactly old world charm.

As one might expect, the major first-class hotels which cater for travelling businesspeople are usually well-equipped with everything their guests might want. Photocopying machines, telex and telefax are fairly standard, and services such as secretarial, translating and interpreting etc. can almost always be arranged (it is a good idea to prearrange during fairs and exhibitions). Conference rooms, often in a variety of different sizes and furnished with screens, overhead projectors, lecterns and microphones etc., are provided by all leading city hotels, and functions from intimate dinners to lavish fashion shows and PR extravaganzas are part of the large hotel scene.

Some hotels provide executive floors and executive suites (which are often almost identical to the other floors and suites, only more expensive). In all western German cities that sport a trade fair, there can be serious accommodation problems during exhibitions. In Frankfurt, for example, there are often no beds available (in hotels of any category or even in private houses) within a radius of 50 km; exhibitors make reservations years in advance. The problem can be even more acute in Berlin during a mammoth fair such as the International Tourism Exchange (ITB). A visitor who is unable to find a room in a city under these circumstances is advised to contact the reservation service of the city tourist office *(Verkehrsamt)* or the booking service of the trade fair itself (for phone numbers, see City Portraits). Hotels in major western German cities are expensive, often exorbitantly so during exhibitions; a single room may cost between DM 250 and DM 500. Corporate rates are occasionally available and should be requested; some hotels offer special weekend packages. Prices are normally quoted without breakfast in the top hotels, and quoted with breakfast in smaller, family run establishments; luxury hotels offer American-style as well as buffet breakfasts in addition to the standard continental roll and coffee, and even simple hotels normally provide a slice of ham and packaged cheese.

Hotel Reservation Services in/for Germany

0130 numbers are charged at the local call rate.

Arabella Hotels	(089) 92 32 44 44
Best Western	(0130) 44 55/(06196) 47 24 10
CARRERA	(069) 42 08 90 89 (bookings for Minotel, Kempinski, Scandic)
Hilton	(0130) 23 45
Holiday Inns International	(0130) 56 78
Hotel Reservation Service (HRS)	(0221) 20 77-0 (HRS publishes an international hotel directory; included are 1,800 hotels in Germany, among them 150 in the new *Länder*)
Intercontinental + Forum Hotels	(0130) 39 55
Hyatt	(0130) 29 29
Kempinski	(06102) 5 00 20
Leading Hotels of the World	(0130) 21 10/(069) 2 99 87 70
Marriott	(0130) 44 22/(069) 7 95 50
Mövenpick	(0130) 22 17
Nikko (via JAL)	(0130) 68 78/(069) 1 36 00
Penta	(069) 59 01 41
Pullman International	(069) 23 08 58
Quality International	(0130) 55 22
Queens Hotels	(0130) 44 33
Ramada	(0130)81 23 40
Resinter	(069) 74 00 41 (bookings for Ibis, Mercure, Novotel)
Ringhotels e.V.	(089) 4 48 92 06
Scandic	(069) 8 00 71 60
Sheraton	(0130) 35 35
Steigenberger (SRS)	(0130) 44 00
Supranational	(0130) 69 69 (bookings for Maritim, Rema, Arabella)
Top International Hotels	(0211) 57 80 75
Trusthouse Forte	(0130) 29 44/(069) 23 91 96

(Note: The German National Tourist Board (DTZ) has a room reservation service: ADZ in Frankfurt, (069) 74 07 67.)

City Portraits

Berlin

By far the largest city in united Germany, the city-state of Berlin covers an area of 883 sq km; it boasts 3.4 million inhabitants and is likely to boast 5 million in the not-so-distant future.

Unknown to many, Berlin has once again been the capital of Germany since 3 October 1990, the day of German unification. The battle between Bonn and Berlin that raged until June 1991 was not to decide which city should be the German capital, but to decide whether Berlin should revert to being the seat of government as well. This rather muddled situation (now resolved: Berlin bags both prizes) is in good keeping with the forty-year pre-unification confusion over the status of Berlin. A city in the middle of East German territory, divided up by the Allies after the war, half of Berlin "belonged" to the West, although it was neither the capital nor even a legal part of the Federal Republic. The other half, meanwhile, was definitely part and parcel (and capital) of East Germany. Now the Wall is down, and Berlin is whole, if not yet entirely hearty. Forty years of division cannot be eliminated overnight, and the contrast between the two Berlins is stark. The repair job on former East Berlin will be massive – and fascinating. Not only do residential areas and historic sites require wholesale restoration, but there are huge barren areas waiting to be developed, and there is already fierce competition among international architects to come up with the best plans to utilize the space.

Berlin has traditionally been a centre of the arts, a cultural Mecca. It hosts a regular schedule of international film festivals, trade fairs and professional conventions. Partly with the help of special incentives provided by the Bonn government, western Berlin manufactures electrical appliances, machinery, garments, optical goods, pharmaceuticals and printed matter. It serves as an alternative headquarters for such major German companies as Schering, Springer and Siemens. The German federal supervisory authorities for health and banking are headquartered in Berlin.

There is little doubt that Berlin will flourish and that its heyday is yet to come. Certainly, its geographical location in the "new" Europe is pivotal. Eventually, and when all of the logistics problems have been sorted out, everybody who is anybody in industry, commerce and finance will have to show off in Berlin, the new European hub. Paris and London, watch out. In the meantime...although the path to setting up new premises in Berlin has not been entirely smooth for Daimler-Benz, and while other lesser companies are hesitating to rush in too precipitously, in the area of tourism, trade is booming. Visitors to the city are advised to book well ahead.

Western Berlin postal code: W-1000; Western Berlin telephone code: 030
Eastern Berlin postal code: O-1000 Berlin; Eastern Berlin telephone code: 00372

Top companies: Daimler-Benz, Siemens, AEG, Schering

Hotels:

Bristol-Hotel Kempinski ****
Kurfürstendamm 27, Berlin 15
Tel: (030) 88 43 40
Fax: (030) 88 36 075

Grand Hotel ****
Friedrichstr. 158, 1080 Berlin (East)
Tel: (00 37 2) 2 09 20
Fax: (00 37 2) 2 29 40 95

Inter-Continental ****
Budapester Str. 2, Berlin 30
Tel: (030) 2 60 20
Fax: (030) 2 60 28 07 60

Steigenberger Hotel ****
Los-Angeles-Platz 1, Berlin 30
Tel: (030) 2 10 80
Fax: (030) 2 10 81 17

Grand Hotel Esplanade ****
Lützowufer 15, Berlin 30
Tel: (030) 26 10 11
Fax: (030) 2 62 91 21

Metropol ****
Friedrichstr. 150, 1080 Berlin (East)
Tel: (00 37 2)) 2 20 40
Fax: (00 37 2) 2 20 42 09

Palace ****
Budapester Str. (Europa Centre),
Berlin 30
Tel: (030) 25 49 70
Fax: (030) 2 62 65 77

Palasthotel ****
Karl-Liebknecht-Str., 1020 Berlin (East)
Tel: (00 37 2) 24 10
Fax: (00 37 2) 2 12 72 73

Recommended sights: Europa Centre, Kurfürstendamm, Brandenburger Tor, Schloß Charlottenburg, Zoo – and former East Berlin

Useful information and phone numbers:
Tourist office: (030) 2 62 60 31
LH (Lufthansa): (030) 8 87 51 (res: 8 87 55)
DB (Deutsche Bundesbahn): (030) 1 94 19
Taxis: (030) 6902
Police: (030) 110
Doctor: (030) 0031
Distance from Tegel airport: 8 km
– Cost of taxi (approx.): DM 20
– Public transportation: DM 2.70

Bonn

Known as the "federal village", Bonn has been the seat of the federal government since 1949, at which time it was hardly more than a suburb of Cologne (27 km away) and former residence of the archbishops of Cologne (who moved out in the 18th century). Never intended as more than a temporary capital until Germany was united and Berlin regained its rightful status, at first Bonn wasn't sure whether to grow into its new position, or simply wait until the government had moved on before going back to sleep. As time passed, buildings had to be erected, communications improved and willy nilly, the village previously renowned only for its university and Beethoven (born there in 1770) became synonymous with the West German government. Slowly but surely, Bonn got used to the importance thrust upon it, and when unification duly (if in the event unexpectedly) became reality, the mini-city (it still has less than 300,000 inhabitants) was thrown into a state of disarray. That it lost its status as capital on Unification Day, well, there was nothing to be done about that, since the constitution was quite firm on the matter. But the seat of government – that was something Bonn was not about to relinquish to Berlin without a fight. The battle raged on until June 1991, with everybody (from members of parliament and public figures to the locals in both cities) taking sides, counting votes, filling daily newspapers and making controversial public speeches. Now that Bonn has lost the fight (by a fairly narrow margin), it will have to take stock and decide where it is heading.

Bonn's future is therefore uncertain. Whatever happens, though, it is not likely to sink back into oblivion; when the government bodies finally move out (and the process will take time), other institutions will probably move in to take advantage of the available space.

Bonn postal code: W-5300; Bonn telephone code: 0228

Hotels:

Günnewig Hotel Bristol ****
Prinz-Albert-Str. 2, Bonn 1
Tel: (0228) 2 69 80
Fax: (0228) 269 82 22

Günnewig Residence Hotel ***
Kaiserplatz 11, Bonn 1
Tel: (0228) 2 69 70
Fax: (0228) 2 69 77 77

Scandic Crown Hotel ***
Berliner Freiheit 2, Bonn 1
Tel: (0228) 7 26 90
Fax: (0228) 7 26 97 00

Pullman-Hotel Königshof ***
Adenauerallee 9, Bonn 1
Tel: (0228) 2 60 10
Fax: (0228) 2 60 15 29

Maritim ****
Godesberger Allee, Bonn 2
Tel: (0228) 8 10 80
Fax: (0228) 8 10 88 11
(at Bonn-Bad Godesberg)

Steigenberger Hotel Venusberg ****
An der Casselsruhe 1, Kessenich 1
Tel: (0228) 28 80
Fax: (0228) 28 82 88
(at Kessenich, 3 km south)

Recommended sights: Althaus, Münster, Freizeitpark Rheinaue, Marktplatz, Beethovenhaus

Useful information and phone numbers:
Tourist office: (0228) 77 34 66
LH (Lufthansa): (0228) 51 91 10
DB (Deutsche Bundesbahn): (0228) 1 94 19
Taxis: (0228) 55 55 55
Police: (0228) 110
Doctor: (0228) 28 01
Distance from Cologne/Bonn airport: 28 km
– Cost of taxi (approx.): DM 50
– Airport bus is free for all ticket holders.

Bremen

The Free Hanseatic City of Bremen sounds, as in the case of Hamburg, imposing and majestic. It isn't. A third of the size of Hamburg, Bremen is a cosier city with character and charm. Like Hamburg (and Berlin), Bremen is a city-state, and together with Bremerhaven, 69 km down the long Weser estuary on the North Sea, forms a remarkable port system. Bremen is the second largest seaport and maritime trading city in the Federal Republic; it is in fact the oldest maritime city, had market rights in the 10th century, became a member of the Hanseatic League in the 14th century and a Free Imperial City in the 17th century. Bremen's heyday was in the 19th century after it started trading with America and became a major cotton and coffee centre; a mammoth project on the shipping channel enabled seagoing vessels to sail up the Weser to the city itself. The 20th century hasn't been quite so kind to Bremen, which has suffered the fate of all shipbuilding, maritime trading cities. Although it has diversified, a concentration on engineering contributed to difficult times in the Eighties and lack of funds prevented leaps into potentially more profitable industrial sectors. Nevertheless, Bremen remains a giant commodities port, and 40% of its population depend on it for their livelihood. Bremen handles nearly 60% of western Germany's incoming raw tobacco and 40% of its imported coffee along with a large proportion of wool, cotton, jute, lumber and citrus imports. As a result, many raw materials are refined in the city-state. Beck's ships its premium beer labelled with the city's crest around the world. The city assembles Mercedes cars, makes steel at the Klöckner mills and in recent decades has also acquired an aerospace industry with MBB-Erno. Bremen exports large amounts of German steel and chemicals. The city-state appears to have entered a new growth phase after a period of above-average unemployment in the mid-Eighties. In per capita domestic product, Bremen ranks second only to Hamburg in standard of living.

Bremen postal code: W-2800; Bremen telephone code: 0421

Top companies: Daimler Benz, Bremer Vulcan, Messerschmidt-Bölkow-Blohm (MBB), Krupp Atlas

Hotels:

Parkhotel ****
Im Bürgerpark, Bremen 1
Tel: (0421) 3 40 80
Fax: (0421) 3 40 86 02

Zur Post (Best Western) ***
Bahnhofsplatz 11, Bremen 1
Tel: (0421) 3 05 90
Fax: (0421) 3 05 95 91

Bremen Marriott ***
Hillmannplatz 20, Bremen 1
Tel: (0421) 1 76 70
Fax: (0421) 1 76 72 38

Mercure - Columbus **
Bahnhofsplatz 5, Bremen 1
Tel: (0421) 1 41 61
Fax: (0421) 1 53 69

Recommended sights: Markt, Böttcherstraße, Schnoorviertel, harbour, Kunsthaus

Useful information and phone numbers:
Tourist office: (0421) 30 80 00
LH (Lufthansa): (0421) 3 60 00 (res: 3 60 06)
DB (Deutsche Bundesbahn): (0421) 19 41
Taxis: (0421) 14 0 14
Police: (0421) 110
Doctor: (0421) 1 92 92
Distance from nearest airport: 3 km
– Cost of taxi (approx.): DM 10
– Public transportation: Tram # 5, DM 2.40

Cologne (Köln)

The oldest of the major German cities, it was given the name "Colonia" by the Romans in A.D. 50 and quickly developed into one of the empire's most important trade and manufacturing centres north of the Alps. Charlemagne (no less) founded the archbishopric of Cologne in 785, and the archbishop of Cologne remained for several centuries one of the most important feudal lords in the Holy Roman Empire. From the 12th to the 15th centuries, Cologne was the most populous and wealthiest city in the German-speaking world, and it wasn't until the New World was discovered and new forms of business and trade routes were opened up that Cologne lost its pre-eminence. With a population of just over one million, Cologne today is the fourth largest city in the Federal Republic and the third largest industrial and commercial centre. Henry Ford helped turn Cologne into a major car manufacturing centre, where five international companies now have their German subsidiaries (it was in Cologne that the four-stroke internal combustion engine was designed in 1876). Chemicals, engineering (electrical, mechanical and precision), insurance and banking are all growth sectors, and with four radio and TV broadcasting companies and over 50 film production enterprises, Cologne already considers itself the hub of the electronic media (the next step in this direction is the planned MediaPark Köln, an information technology centre to be created on the 200,000 sq metre site of the old railway freight terminal). The trade fair attracts 1.5 million visitors to its up to 35 fairs; to accommodate all of the business visitors and tourists, the city is adding as fast as it can to its present around 15,000 hotel beds. "A focal point of Western culture" (Baedeker), noted for everything from sports to its research institutes, Cologne has every right to be smug, and it is. The mighty cathedral towers above the largely rebuilt inner city, the old town is the most extensive in Germany, and even the railway station is impressive. Add a touch of Eau de Cologne (first made by Italian chemist in the early 18th century) and the city is irresistible.

Cologne postal code: W-5000; Cologne telephone code: 0221

Top companies: Esso, Shell, Ford, Gerling-Konzern

Hotels:

Excelsior Hotel Ernst ****
Trankgasse 1 (Domplatz), Köln 1
Tel: (0221) 27 01
Fax: (0221) 13 51 50

Inter-Continental ****
Helenenstr. 14, Köln 1
Tel: (0221) 22 80
Fax: (0221) 2 28 13 01

Hyatt Regency ****
Kennedy-Ufer 2a, Köln 21
Tel: (0221) 8 28 12 34
Fax: (0221) 8 28 13 70

Maritim ****
Heumarkt 20, Köln 1
Tel: (0221) 2 02 70
Fax: (0221) 2 02 78 26

Dom Hotel ****
Domklosterstr. 2a, Köln 1
Tel: (0221) 23 37 51
Fax: (0221) 2 02 42 60

Hotel im Wasserturm ***
Kaygasse 2, Köln 1
Tel: (0221) 2 00 80
Fax: (0221) 2 00 88 88

Recommended sights: Cathedral, Altstadt (old town), Roman-Germanic Museum, Wallraf-Richartz Museum, Museum Ludwig

Useful information and phone numbers:
Tourist office: (0221) 2 21 33 45
(Trade fair room bookings: (0221) 8 21 22 73)
LH (Lufthansa): (0221) 2 08 24
DB (Deutsche Bundesbahn): (0221) 14 11
Taxis: (0221) 28 82
Police: (0221) 110, Doctor: (0221) 72 07 72
Distance from nearest airport: 18 km,
– Cost of taxi (approx.): DM 30
– Airport bus: DM 3.60

Dresden

It is one of the truly sad testimonials to the spiritual poverty of the East German regime that it considered Dresden to be a showcase city. It was a model of "socialist industry, a centre of science and technology, a place of culture and the new socialist art...an attraction for international tourism" according to one city plaque (which may now have been removed). The city that was once an architectural jewel was devastated by an Anglo-American bomb attack in February 1945. Thereafter, many of the "decadent" treasures that survived the raid were left to crumble and rot, or razed to the ground (as in the case of the famous baroque street Rampische Strasse) to make room for the new socialist art: concrete prison-like residential blocks or factories. Only a handful of historically significant buildings were restored (many years after the war, when the era of "socialist reconstruction" had been replaced by that of "national cultural heritage"), and these have already been so blackened by air pollution that it is hard to believe that the restoration of the Semper Opera (for example) was not completed until 1985.

Once-beautiful Dresden, known as the Florence of the Elbe because of the baroque profile given to it by August the Strong in the 17th century, is once again the capital of Saxony and once again a showcase. In the past year, this city of just over half a million has come to represent the past, present and future of eastern German cities – a microcosm in a macrocosm. The world is pouring into Dresden to learn about and assess the eastern German situation. Congresses, conferences, symposia are all being scheduled for Dresden. The result: a severe lack of accommodation and all other business and tourist facilities. Moreover, both air and rail transportation are overstrained – at times, the quickest way in or out of Dresden is via Leipzig, 130 km away. Visitors should plan well ahead or be prepared to stay outside the city.

Dresden postal code: O-8020; Dresden telephone code: 00 37 51

Hotels:

Bellevue ****
Köpckestr. 15, Dresden
Tel: (00 37 51) 5 66 20
Fax: (00 37 51) 5 59 97

Dresdener Hof ****
An der Frauenkirche 5, Dresden

Tel: (00 37 51) 4 84 10
Fax: (00 37 51) 4 84 17 00

Lilienstein / Königstein **
Prager Str., Dresden
Tel: (00 37 51) 4 85 60
Telex: (00 37 51) 2-6 165

Recommended sights: Zwinger, Altmarkt, Frauenkirche, Brühlsche Terrasse

Useful information and phone numbers:
Tourist office: (00 37-51) 4 59 50 25
LH (Lufthansa): (00 37 51) 5 66 2-294 (res: 58 31 41-45)
DR (Reichsbahn): (00 37 51) 4 61 36 52
Taxis: (00 37 51) 459 81
Police: (00 37 51) 5 94 00
Doctor: (00 37 51) 4 31 98 20
Distance from nearest airport: 14 km
– Cost of taxi (approx.): DM 20

Düsseldorf

Düsseldorf has carefully chosen an image for itself; the incarnation of the success and prosperity of the Federal Republic, a forward-looking "new" town, aggressive, smart and cosmopolitan. A wise choice, because in terms of history, tradition and size, it cannot really compete with nearby Cologne. Not that Düsseldorf has no past; 1988 was the year of its 700th birthday as a city (an honour conferred upon it by Count Adolf von Berg in 1288). After the Berg family died out in the 17th century, Düsseldorf enjoyed a brief period as the capital of the electors of the Neuburg-Palatinate and became a centre of the arts; its fortunes in the 18th century were mixed, but it had a brief flare of glory following the French Revolution when Napoleon made it into the capital of the Grand Duchy of Berg. After becoming Prussian in 1815, Düsseldorf moved along slowly with the tide, but nothing really significant happened until 1946, when the state of Nordrhein-Westfalen was created and Düsseldorf made into its capital. Düsseldorf is in the process of revising itself. For years it thrived as the administrative centre for the major Rhine industries, and shared their fortunes. And their tribulations. To offset the recession, Düsseldorf has diversified energetically; it has already established itself as an important financial centre; has shifted emphasis from engineering to electronics; has encouraged the development of service industries. In the race to attract foreign companies, Düsseldorf is the national champion, outdoing its nearest rival (Frankfurt) two to one. Over 3,000 non-German businesses are using the city as their administrative home-away-from-home, and this, of course, enhances the city's international flair. Düsseldorf is particularly proud of its almost DM 200 million Japan Centre, housing 300 Japanese companies (every hundredth Düsseldorfer is Japanese), but in the scramble to attract Far Eastern partners, the city has just lost out to Frankfurt in a bid to represent the commercial and banking interests of the

People's Republic of China. And Düsseldorf is none too happy that Frankfurt is also scoring well with Japanese banks. With its wide, tree-lined streets, its elegant shops and boutiques, and above all, its well-dressed people, Düsseldorf considers itself to be one of Europe's smartest cities. The Michelin Guide calls Düsseldorf a "setter of sartorial fashion", and fashion shows – not just sartorial – are frequent (sometimes impromptu in the Königsallee ("Kö"), the Berliner Allee and in Schadowstraße).

Düsseldorf postal code: W-4000; Düsseldorf telephone code: 0211

Top companies: Daimler-Benz, Henkel, Krupp, Salzgitter, Thyssen, Mannesmann

Hotels:

Breidenbacher Hof *****
Heinrich-Heine-Allee 36, Düsseldorf 1
Tel: (0211) 30 30; 86 01
Fax: (0211) 30 38 30

Nikko ****
Immermannstr. 41, Düsseldorf 1
Tel: (0211) 83 40
Fax: (0211) 16 12 16

Steigenberger Parkhotel ****
Corneliusplatz 1, Düsseldorf 1
Tel: (0211) 1 38 10
Fax: (0211) 13 16 79

Hilton ****
Georg-Glock-Str. 20, Düsseldorf 30
Tel: (0211) 4 37 70
Fax: (0211) 43 77 654

Holiday Inn ***
Düsseldorf Königsallee
Graf-Adolf-Platz 10, Düsseldorf 1
Tel: (0211) 3 87 30
Fax: (0211) 3 87 33 90

Recommended sights: Königsallee (Kö), Hofgarten with Schloß Jägerhof, Altstadt (old town), museums, Heinrich Heine Haus

Useful information and phone numbers:
Tourist office: (0211) 35 05 05
LH (Lufthansa): (0211) 13 21 68 (res: 88 85)
DB (Deutsche Bundesbahn): (0211) 1 94 19
Taxis: (0211) 3 33 33
Police: (0211) 110

Doctor: (0211) 1 92 92
Distance from nearest airport: 11 km
– Cost of taxi (approx.): DM 16
– Public transportation: S-Bahn, DM 4.80

Essen

The capital of the Ruhr, western Germany's fifth largest city (a gratuitous honour, since four other cities have an almost identical number of inhabitants), Essen is not the ugly, black city one might suppose, given its smoke-stack past. It is unquestionably an industrial city, and has been since the early 19th century. Today, it is the headquarters of a number of large corporations, including Ruhrkohle AG, Germany's largest coal-mining enterprise, and RWE, Europe's largest electricity company; however, Essen's coal mines have long been closed, its steel production severely hit, and no blast furnaces or steelworks have been restarted in the immediate vicinity of the city since the end of the last war. Essen has progressively and rapidly been going "soft", moving from heavy production into electronics and design. The giants (Krupp, Thyssen, Hochtief, AEG, Siemens, etc.) are still around; in fact, 11 of Germany's biggest companies have their headquarters in the city, but more and more dynamic, small enterprises are entering the Essen arena. Essen's trade fairs do not compete with the extravaganzas in Hanover, Cologne or Frankfurt, but they still attract a sizeable number of visitors every year. Not an outstandingly beautiful city, Essen manages to hold its own and has its share of green surroundings including the lovely Grugapark, 70 hectares of land laid out for the Ruhr Horticultural Show in 1929 and enlarged since. Add to the parks and gardens some elegant shops and a variety of cultural institutions, and Essen becomes more interesting than its reputation suggests. (The 1986 Rand McNally New Century World Atlas consistently names Essen as the largest city in Germany. Presumably, Essen is being attributed with the population of the entire Ruhr conurbation, including Dortmund, Duisburg, Bochum, Recklinghausen and sur-rounding areas).

Essen postal code: W-4300; Essen telephone code: 0201

Top companies: Krupp, Thyssen, Hochtief, AEG, Ruhrgas, Siemens, Karstadt, Axel Springer

Hotels:

Sheraton ****
Huyssenallee 55, Essen 1
Tel: (0201) 2 09 51
Fax: (0201) 23 11 73

Handelshof - Mövenpick ***
Am Hauptbahnhof 2, Essen 1
Tel: (0201) 1 70 80
Fax: (0201) 1 70 81 73

Essener Hof **
Teichstr. 2, Essen 1

Tel: (0201) 2 09 01
Fax: (0201) 23 83 51

Bredeney (Scandic Crown Hotel) ****
Theodor-Althoff-Str. 5, Essen 1
Tel: (0201) 76 90
Fax: (0201) 7 69 31 43

Schloß Hugenpoet ***
August-Thyssen-Str. 51, Essen 18
Tel: (02054) 60 54
Fax: (02054) 12 04 50

Recommended sights: Münster (cathedral), Folkwang Museum, Villa Hügel, Grugapark, Baldeneysee, old town centres in Werden and Kettwig

Useful information and phone numbers:
Tourist office: (0201) 7 24 44 01
LH (Lufthansa): (0201) 4 28 71-4
DB (Deutsche Bundesbahn): (0201) 7 99 74 21 - 23
Taxis: (0201) 77 80 80
Police: (0201) 110
Doctor: (0201) 7 99 11
Distance from nearest airport (Düsseldorf): 30 km
– Cost of taxi (approx.): DM 35
– Public transportation: Bus or S-Bahn via Düsseldorf, DM 6.20

Frankfurt

The city internationally known for its sausages is vastly underrated, even (or particularly) by its inhabitants, who sheepishly protest that it isn't all that bad. The news of Frankfurt's increasing importance as a major (if not in size) European city is no longer classified, however, and is filtering down to the Frankfurters themselves. The last native who appreciated his home town seems to have been Goethe, who in the late 18th century already recognized it as "the secret capital". And capital of the Federal Republic it could have become; since it was the traditional coronation city for a succession of emperors from 1562 to 1806, the seat of the Federal Diet from 1815 to 1866, and in 1848/49, the location of the first German National Assembly (in the Paulskirche), it was an obvious candidate to replace Berlin in 1949. Fate (or rather Adenauer) decreed it otherwise, and Frankfurt continued to go about its business – dealing with money. "A breeding ground for financiers" says the Michelin, and this is undoubtedly true. Granted the right in the 16th century to mint money, Frankfurt became a thriving banking city with an international reputation even before Rothschild and his sons ("the five Frankfurters") left their mark in banking history. Today, Frankfurt is home to the Bundesbank (the German central bank). Close to 400 banks, native and foreign, are represented in the city, and the figure seems to be going up by the day. Not surprisingly, the Frankfurt stock exchange is number one in Germany, and Frankfurt is the nation's wealthiest city. Frankfurt has a few healthy industries which add to its prosperity: chemicals, machine tools and electrical products head the list. Its trade fair is eminent, if not yet pre-eminent in the Federal Republic, and attracts around 2 million visitors per year. The fair grounds have been vastly improved and enlarged in recent years, and the newly built *Messeturm* (fair tower) is, at 256 metres, the tallest building in Europe. Other skyscrapers now in the planning stage will contribute to the "Mainhattan" skyline in the Nineties. Frankfurt was badly damaged during the war, patched together in appalling taste in the Fifties, and has been undergoing steady cosmetic surgery for the past decade. There are already distinct signs that the patient may be quite presentable if the doctors ever finish their work. In a study prepared for the EC Commission, of 103 European cities surveyed, Frankfurt was declared to be the "best" place to live with regard to environment, income, facilities, social conditions and the like. Attractive to live in and also to set up business in, Frankfurt is home to an increasing number of international companies.

Frankfurt postal code: W-6000; Frankfurt telephone code: 069

Top companies: Deutsche Bundesbank and all banks, Hoechst, Metallgesellschaft, AEG (part of Daimler-Benz), Degussa, Philipp Holzmann

Hotels:

Frankfurter Hof (Steigenberger) ****
Kaiserplatz 17, Frankfurt 1
Tel: (069) 2 15 02
Fax.: (069) 21 59 00

Inter-Continental ****
Wilhelm-Leuschner-Str. 43, Frankfurt 1
Tel: (069) 23 05 61
Fax: (069) 25 24 67

Hessischer Hof ****
Friedrich-Ebert-Anlage 40, Frankfurt 1
Tel: (069) 7 54 00
Fax: (069) 7 54 09 24

Marriott ****
Hamburger Allee 2, Frankfurt 90

Tel: (069) 7 95 50
Fax: (069) 79 55 24 32

Park Hotel ***
Wiesenhüttenplatz 28, Frankfurt 1
Tel: (069) 2 69 70
Fax: (069) 26 97 88 49

Recommended sights: Römerberg, Goethehaus, Alt-Sachsenhausen, Museumsufer (the museums on the south bank of the Main)

Useful information and phone numbers:
Tourist office: (069) 21 23 88 00
LH (Lufthansa): (069) 69 01 (res: (069) 23 06 21)
DB (Deutsche Bundesbahn): (069) 23 05 21
Taxis: (069) 23 00 01; 25 00 01
Police: (069) 110
Doctor: (069) 1 15 00
Distance from nearest airport: 11 km
– Cost of taxi (approx.): DM 35
– Public transportation: S-Bahn, DM 3.30

Hamburg

The Free Hanseatic City of Hamburg sounds and is majestic. A state (*Land*) in its own right, western Germany's second largest city (1.6 million inhabitants) sits imposingly at the head of the long mouth of the river Elbe and is a major European (indeed, world) port despite its distance from the open sea (110 km/68 miles). Although founded in the 9th century and with a long Hanseatic tradition, visually, Hamburg is a city of the 19th and 20th centuries – mainly because about one third of the inner districts (including part of the port) were wiped out a hundred years later during Hitler's war. During the postwar reconstruction, many of the more interesting buildings were restored, and a lot has been done since to preserve and enhance the beauty of the city. The Außenalster, a lake in the centre of town large enough to go sailing on, is quite magnificent.

Hamburg owes its prosperity to its port and its commerce. Its shipping heyday was in the 19th century, when American independence and the emergence of Latin America led to an enormous expansion of the city's industries and trade.

Today, the deep-water port handles 40 capital ships a day, almost 14,000 a year, and around 50 million metric tonnes of cargo annually. Hamburg has built a huge container port, which has succeeded in the past decade in snaring a large share of Europe's fast-growing container traffic with the Far East. Hamburg's overall container traffic now approaches 2 million "twenty-foot" containers.

But in addition to being a true harbour city (famous for its sailors, red-light districts and early-morning fish markets), Hamburg has shown in recent years that it can be versatile; to make up for the decline in shipbuilding, heavy engineering and other port-related activities, it has branched out very successfully into high-tech industries. In areas such as chemicals, cosmetics, foodstuffs, brewing and cigarette manufacture, Hamburg's importance has long been established, and its banks and insurance companies are thriving. More importantly, Hamburg prides itself on being the "Media Capital" of Germany, a printing and publishing city which produces 40% of the country's magazines and newspapers. Hamburg is a serious city, the cultural centre of northern Germany. It has a distinguished intellectual history, and in the 18th century Klopstock, Lessing and Matthias Claudius were among its more renowned literati. Hamburg is an academic city, with excellent research institutions and universities. Above all, it is an internationally minded city, and with around 2,500 importers and exporters, claims to be the largest foreign trading centre in the Federal Republic. Several of the biggest multinational oil companies have their German headquarters here. The city's per capita domestic product of over DM 57,000 is the highest of any German *Land*.

The people of Hamburg are said (by the people of Munich) to be stiff and reserved, but they have their own, quiet way about them which makes them no less friendly, given time.

Hamburg postal code: W-2000; Hamburg telephone code: 040

Top companies: Blohm & Voss, Howaldtswerke, MBB, Philips, Valvo, LH (technical service), BP, Conoco, Esso, Mobil, Shell, BAT, Unilever, Gruner + Jahr

Hotels:

Atlantic Hotel Kempinski *****
An der Alster 7, Hamburg 1
Tel: (040) 2 88 80
Fax: (040) 24 71 29

Vier Jahreszeiten *****
Neuer Jungfernstieg 9,
2000 Hamburg 36
Tel: (040) 3 49 40
Fax: (040) 3 49 46 02

Ramada Renaissance ****
Große Bleichen, Hamburg 36
Tel: (040) 34 91 80
Fax: (040) 34 91 84 31

Inter-Continental ****
Frontenay 10, Hamburg 36

Tel: (040) 41 41 50
Fax: (040) 41 41 51 82

SAS Plaza Hotel Hamburg ****
Marseiller Str. 2, Hamburg 36
Tel: (040) 3 50 20
Fax: (040) 35 02 33 33

Recommended sights: Alster Lake, Rathaus (town hall), Altstadt (old town), port, Warehouse Town, St. Michaelis, St. Pauli/Reeperbahn, Fish Market (Sundays), Kunsthalle, Planten un Blomen (park)

Useful information and phone numbers:
Tourist office: (040) 30 05 10
LH (Lufthansa): (040) 3 59 50 (res: 3 59 55)
DB (Deutsche Bundesbahn): (040) 19419
Taxis: (040) 7 34 05 82
Police: (040) 110
Doctor: (040) 19214
Distance from nearest airport: 13 km
– Cost of taxi (approx.): DM 25
– Airport City Bus: DM 2.80

Hanover (Hannover)

To some, the name Hanover conjures up a modern German city, the capital of Niedersachsen and an important economic centre; to others, it conjures up the British royal family. In 1714, the Elector Georg of Hanover became King George I of England. The court moved to London, and Britain and Hanover were ruled by one sovereign until 1837, when Salic Law prevented Queen Victoria from succeeding to the House of Hanover throne. Her uncle Ernst-Augustus took over and the House of Hanover flourished until the Prussians annexed the kingdom in 1866 and turned Hanover into a provincial Prussian capital. There is little left in Hanover today to recall the royal battles of old. The Second World War destroyed over half of the city and 85% of the centre; the royal palace of Herrenhausen did not survive, although the gardens have been beautifully restored. Modern Hanover is a well-planned, convenient city which owes its international reputation to its annual industrial trade fair held every April. The Hannover Messe is billed as the "Fair of

Fairs" and attracts almost as many visitors as the city has inhabitants. The influx of transients strains the city's services to the utmost; although many new hotels have relieved accommodation problems, there always seems to be a room shortage. The situation is not quite as acute during the other fairs held throughout the year, but the best time to visit Hanover (if one has a choice) is during a fair lull, when the pace is less hectic and the hospitality warmer. Hanover is having its industrial trials and tribulations; unemployment is high, in part due to overdependence on the car industry which has been on the decline in the area in recent years, as has the construction machinery sector, another mainstay of Hanover industry. Nevertheless, rubber and records are doing well and the city is diversifying into marine and space research, communications and the service industries.

Hanover postal code: W-3000; Hanover telephone code: 0511

Top companies: Continental, Varta, VDO, Hanomag

Hotels:

Inter-Continental ****
Friedrichswall 11, Hannover 1
Tel: (0511) 1 69 11
Fax: (0511) 32 51 95

Karstens Hotel Luisenhof ****
Luisenstr. 1-3, Hannover 1
Tel: (0511) 1 24 40
Fax: (0511) 3 04 48 07

Schweizerhof ***
Hinüberstr. 6, Hannover 1

Tel: (0511) 3 49 50
Fax: (0511) 3 49 51 23

Maritim ***
Hildesheimer Str. 34, Hannover 1
Tel: (0511) 1 65 31
Fax: (0511) 88 48 46

Landhaus Ammann ***
Hildesheimer Str. 185, Hannover 1
Tel: (0511) 83 08 18
Fax: (0511) 8 43 77 49

Recommended sights: City-Centre Kröpcke, Altes Rathaus (old town hall), Leineschloß, museums, Eilenriede (municipal woods)

Useful information and phone numbers:
Tourist office: (0511) 1 68 23 19
LH (Lufthansa): (0511) 3 10 50 (res: 3 10 55)
DB (Deutsche Bundesbahn): (0511) 6 11 11

Taxis: (0511) 38 11; 21 43
Police: (0511) 110
Doctor: (0511) 31 40 44
Distance from nearest airport: 12 km
– Cost of taxi (approx.): DM 25
– Public transportation: Bus, DM 4.60
– Air taxi service from airport to fairgrounds: Luftreederei Marato, tel: 89 27 25

Leipzig

Leipzig, currently home to some 550,000 souls, used to be the second largest GDR city after Berlin. It is (slightly) more populous and of considerably greater economic importance than Dresden, the regional capital. Leipzig has a long history dating back to the Middle Ages when it became a major trading centre and the only market town within a radius of 120 km (by decree of Emperor Maximilian I). Leipzig University, founded in 1409, is one of Germany's oldest, and the Leipzig Fair dates back to 1497. The list of famous people associated with Leipzig is impressive and includes the likes of Luther and Johann Sebastian Bach. The "city of books" has a centuries-old publishing tradition, and will now have to compete with Frankfurt as the national book centre (there is some talk of dividing up the annual autumn book fair between the two cities).

Leipzig supposedly "did well" under the communist regime; it was certainly a showcase city, an iron and steel industrial centre which produced heavy plant and machinery and an international trade fair city visited by people from all over the world. And yet, showcase or not, it too was allowed to go to rack and ruin. As in Dresden, a large section of the city centre was destroyed during the war; there were some attempts at reconstruction on the part of the communists, but for the most part, the regime continued the work of the bombs. Most of Leipzig today is in an appalling state – and it may be too late to save the few historical buildings that still exist.

There are hotels in Leipzig, but only one in the luxury class, and the rest are in need of modernization and sprucing-up. Needless to say, there are not enough guest rooms to cover demand, especially during fairs or congresses. Almost all flights in and out of Leipzig are via Frankfurt and tend to be overbooked.

Leipzig postal code: O-7010; Leipzig telephone code: 00 37 41

Hotels:

Merkur ****
Gerberstr. 15, Leipzig
Tel: (00 37 41) 79 90
Fax: (00 37 41) 7 99 12 29

Stadt Leipzig **
Richard-Wagner-Str. 1-9, Leipzig
Tel: (00 37 41) 28 88 14
Fax: (00 37 41) 28 40 37

Astoria ***
Platz der Republik 2, Leipzig
Tel: (00 37 41) 72 20 0

Recommended sights: Altes Rathaus (old town hall), Nikolaikirche, Thomaskirche, various museums

Useful information and phone numbers:
Tourist office: (00 37 41) 20 02 21
LH (Lufthansa): (00 37 41) 75 96
DR (Reichsbahn): (00 37 41) 7 24 33 60
Taxis: (00 37 41) 2 31 20 52
Police: (00 37 41) 7250
Doctor: (00 37 41) 70936
Distance from nearest airport: 12 km
− Cost of taxi (approx.): DM 35
− Public transportation: DM 4

Munich (München)

From a small 9th century village close to some Benedictine monks (monks = Mönche = München) to the third largest and most expensive western German city, Munich has both made it and has it made; capital of Bayern, pearl of the south and super-centre of culture and kitsch, it is the city most western Germans dream of living in (even those who have never set foot in the place). An architectural riot of rococo, 19th century Greek and 20th century modern, with a touch of late Gothic and Art Nouveau here and there, Munich is still rather gorgeous, a pampered child which has always had the best of everything (including skilful face-lifting and restoration after the Second World War). For all its whimsicality and "I love Bavaria" buttons, Munich is a city to be reckoned with. It is indisputably the number one southern German centre for industry and commerce, and in manufacturing output and "soft" industries (fashion, advertising, printing), it is number one nationwide. Moreover, its star is still rising, since the future industrial prosperity of the country is likely to emanate primarily from the south. Bavaria's late premier, Franz Josef Strauß, was worried that his state and capital would lose some of their prestige in a United Europe, and since according to the Basic Law a state may not secede, he was all in favour of strengthening the principle of federalism and increasing the sovereign powers of the states.

Munich (and its gorgeous surroundings) is a magnet; businesspeople flock to its trade fairs, congresses and exhibitions. Other visitors come for more frivolous reasons: the annual Oktoberfest (in September) and Fasching (carnival). Many come just to see the city and find out if the people in apparent fancy dress (short leather pants, loden jackets and feather-bedecked hats) are for real. (They are.) The present airport, Munich Riem, is far too small for the ever increasing traffic and will give way to a new airport at Erding, 30 km from the city, in 1993. This development will make available to Munich-based businesses and exhibitions valuable land close to the city (Riem being 8 km away), thereby releasing even more valuable land in the centre of town for new development.

Munich postal code: W-8000; Munich telephone code: 089

Top companies: Siemens, BMW, Deutsche Airbus, MBB, Motorola, Texas Instruments, Allianz, Münchner Rück

Hotels:

Vier Jahreszeiten Kempinski ****
Maximilianstr. 17, München 22
Tel: (089) 23 03 90
Fax: (089) 23 03 96 93

Bayerischer Hof
mit Palais Mont Gelas ****
Promenadeplatz 2, München 2
Tel: (089) 2 12 00
Fax: (089) 2 12 09 06

Park-Hilton ****
Am Tucherplatz 7, München 22

Tel: (089) 3 84 50
Fax: (089) 38 45 18 45

Königshof ****
Karlsplatz 25, München 2
Tel: (089) 55 13 60
Fax: (089) 55 13 61 13

Grand Hotel Continental ***
Max-Joseph-Str. 5, München 2
Tel: (089) 55 15 70
Fax: (089) 55 15 75 00

Recommended sights: Marienplatz, Frauenkirche, Residenz, Wittelsbacher Brunnen, Ludwigstraße, Schwabing district, English Garden, museums and galeries, Nymphenburger Schloß and Park

Useful information and phone numbers:
Tourist office: (089) 2 39 11
LH (Lufthansa): (089) 5 11 30 (res: 5 11 38)
DB (Deutsche Bundesbahn): (089) 12 80
Taxis: (089) 2 16 11
Police: (089) 21 41
Doctor: (089) 55 86 61
Distance form nearest airport (Riem): 8 km
– Cost of taxi (approx.): DM 25
– Airport shuttle-bus: DM 5

Stuttgart

Beautifully situated without being particularly beautiful itself, Stuttgart owes most of its history to the Württemberg dynasty, whose members kept coming and going until the middle of the 18th century, at which time they decided to stay. With the advent of the railway a century later, Stuttgart chugged its way into industrialization while clinging on to its agricultural heritage; to this day, Stuttgarters boast that grapes are harvested within 250 metres of the main railway station. The 19th century also saw the flourishing of educational institutions which produced such disparate talents as Schiller, Hegel, Robert Bosch and Gottfried Daimler. The latter was an engineer who invented new-fangled motors and who, in 1901, put on the market a car christened Mercedes (after the daughter of one of his best agents). In 1926, Daimler got together with Carl Benz, who in 1899 had already sold his 2,999th car and become the world's leading auto manufacturer. Together, they established Stuttgart as a high-quality automobile centre, and it still is. (Porsche manufactures luxury sports cars nearby.) Engineering (automotive, electrical and mechanical) accounts for 80% of Stuttgart's industry; chemicals, textiles and above all publishing (with approximately 200 companies) top up the list. Stuttgart is not a major fair city (in terms of size, the fair is small), but it hosts several important events each year. A congress centre is due to be opened in 1991. It might not please either Stuttgart or Düsseldorf to be compared to each other, but the exercise is tempting. Both cities have roughly the same-sized population, both are "new" compared to the geographically relatively close historical and cultural giants, Munich and Cologne respectively, and both have to try harder. Both do. Stuttgart may not yet have the cultural stature of Munich, but it may get there; with two universities, an academy of fine arts and another of music and drama as well as other specialized learning institutes, the city is continuing its tradition of excellence in education. It is home to the internationally acclaimed Stuttgart Ballet and the Stuttgart Chamber Orchestra and has a number of outstanding museums, theatres and choirs. And Stuttgart's Swabian cuisine is in a class all its own.

Stuttgart postal code: W-7000; Stuttgart telephone code: 0711

Top companies: Daimler-Benz, Porsche, Bosch, SEL, Bauknecht, IBM, Nixdorf, Hollzbrinckgruppe, Klett, Deutsche Verlagsanstalt

Hotels:

Steigenberger Hotel Graf Zeppelin ****
Arnulf-Klett-Platz 7, Stuttgart 1
Tel: (0711) 29 98 81
Fax: (0711) 29 21 41

Inter-Continental ****
Neckarstr. 60, Stuttgart 1
Tel: (0711) 2 02 00
Fax: (0711) 20 20 12

Hotel Am Schloßgarten ***
Schillerstr. 23, Stuttgart 1

Tel: (0711) 29 99 11
Fax: (0711) 2 02 68 88

Park Hotel ***
Villastr. 21, Stuttgart 1
Tel: (0711) 28 01 61
Fax: (0711) 28 43 53

Intercity-Hotel ***
Arnulf-Klett-Platz 2, Stuttgart 1
Tel: (0711) 29 98 01
Fax: (0711) 2 26 18 99

Recommended sights: Altes Schloß, Neues Schloß, Stiftskirche, museums

Useful information and phone numbers:
Tourist office: (0711) 2 22 82 40
LH (Lufthansa): (0711) 2 04 41 (res: 2 04 47)
DB (Deutsche Bundesbahn): (0711) 1 94 19
Taxis: (0711) 56 60 61
Police: (0711) 110
Doctor: (0711) 28 02 11
Distance from nearest airport: 14 km
– Cost of taxi (approx.): DM 32,
– Public transportation: Bus A (25 mins.), DM 6

Traffic on the motorways may often come to a standstill, and train delays are no longer unheard-of, but western Germany still has one of the world's finest transportation networks – while the new *Länder* have a lot of catching up to do. Getting from point A to point B in eastern Germany is not an easy matter, especially if one of those points is Berlin, where access roads can hardly cope with the increased post-unification traffic. But help is on the way, now that Transport Minister Günther Krause (one of the few eastern Germans with a cabinet-level post in the new Germany) has set about upgrading and expanding existing infrastructure. Current plans call for nine new railway lines, seven *Autobahn* (motorway) routes and two canals. Since the Wall disappeared from the landscape, the two German railway systems – the western Deutsche Bundesbahn (DB) and the eastern Deutsche Reichsbahn (DR) – have been playing the tricky game of timetable coordination. The adjustments have kept logistics experts working nights, for most DR lines are neither electrified nor built for two-way train traffic.

Western Germany is also dotted with airports connecting all the major cities and a number of minor ones. All the main big-city airports offer direct worldwide flights. East of the Elbe, travellers can now jet to a greater number of destinations throughout western Germany and Europe, often via Frankfurt or Stuttgart – but it will take years before eastern German airports meet western standards.

Air Services and Airports

By far the largest and most important of western Germany's international airports is **Frankfurt Rhine/Main.** With direct flights to 220 cities in 99 countries and a passenger volume of 29.6 million in 1990 (up 11% from 1989), Frankfurt is not just the hub of western Germany, but also of continental Europe. And Rhine/Main continues to expand: by the end of 1994 a new terminal will be completed, with the capacity to serve another 10 to 12 million passengers. By the year 2000, Frankfurt should be catering for almost 38 million travellers a year. In 1990, Berlin was the destination of 40% of inner-German flights. Frankfurt's air cargo centre, stretching over 110 hectares, is Europe's leader, handling 1.2 million tonnes in

1990. Frankfurt airport is a mini-city, with everything from shops, cafés and banks to an emergency clinic, a police station and a non-denominational church; all in all, the airport has 41,000 employees and is also Lufthansa's home base. It features the best airport conference centre in Germany, with facilities designed for every business need (including translation and secretarial services) and the latest in communications technology (including facilities for worldwide video conferences). For information call (069) 6 90-7 05 00.

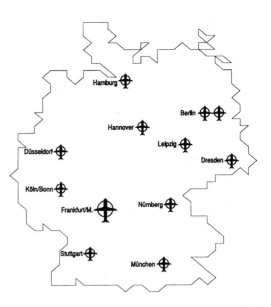

Düsseldorf-Lohausen airport, second in the German airport hierarchy, poses no threat to Frankfurt. It handled almost 12 million passengers in 1990, half of whom flew on charter airlines. With regularly scheduled flights to 80 cities worldwide and an additional 84 holiday destinations, Düsseldorf is the main gateway for over 12 million inhabitants of the Rhine-Ruhr area. Each week, 457 jets take off on domestic routes. In freight, Düsseldorf ranked third after Frankfurt and Cologne/Bonn, processing over 95,000 tonnes in 1990. In 1989, a 200-bed airport hotel with conference rooms for up to 190 people was opened.

Munich-Riem is Germany's third largest airport in passenger volume (almost 11.5 million last year, including more than three million vacationers) and offers direct services to around 40 cities abroad and 15 at home. But its days are numbered, for Munich's new Franz Josef Strauß airport is due to open in May 1992. It is located about 30 kilometres from central Munich and, with a dual runway system, will be able to handle 12 to 14 million passengers a year. Today, Munich-Riem ranks fifth in cargo capacity with air freight amounting to almost 57,000 tonnes in 1990. The Munich Air Cargo Centre at the new airport is designed to handle 250,000 tonnes a year, which can be expanded by 60,000 tonnes annually to a maximum of 1 million. The new airport will house a shopping and service arcade featuring travel agencies, a chemist, banks, restaurants with meeting facilities and a post office for the expected 35,000 daily passengers and over 12,000 airport employees. It is hoped that the new airport will ease the congestion at Frankfurt (although sceptics are not convinced).

All of the other western German airports are relatively small. **Cologne/Bonn** offers scheduled services to only 36 cities. The best connections to eastern Germany are routed via Berlin. There are two-a-day flights to Dresden, one-a-day to Leipzig. Cologne/Bonn is a leading charter hub and is likely to become far more so as the larger airports try to reduce non-scheduled flights in an attempt to deal with rapidly increasing regular traffic. Moreover, the next-closest airport, Düsseldorf, has difficulties expanding, due to its location. In 1990, Cologne/Bonn handled 3.1 million passengers and with 170,000 tonnes of cargo, it was second only to Frankfurt in freight volume.

Hamburg is now coping with almost 7 million passengers yearly, and is too small for the volume. It is being expanded and modernized, however, and in 1993 will be able to handle 12 to 14 million passengers annually. By then freight capacity should reach 220,000 to 250,000 tonnes. Freight volume in 1990 amounted to 88,000 tonnes, with the Far East accounting for about 40% of overall business.

Stuttgart has just completed a badly needed extension: on Easter Sunday 1991, it opened a new passenger terminal (the old one dated back to 1935 and was designed for only 150,000 passengers a year) and the lengthened runways were ready for take-off. Stuttgart offers direct flights to 25 foreign cities and catered for 4.3 million passengers in 1990, with a freight volume of 63,000 tonnes. Connections to eastern Germany have improved: Dresden is served three to five times a day, Leipzig one to three times, Berlin 12 times a day.

Berlin boasts three airports (Tegel, Tempelhof and Schönefeld), all of which are bursting at the seams, with 450 daily flights doubling pre-unification air traffic volume. Lufthansa expects air travel to increase from 9 million passengers yearly to about 17 million by 1995. Tegel saw 6.7 million passengers last year. A new terminal will boost capacity by 3 million as of summer 1992. For the time being, Tegel together with the smaller Tempelhof are carrying the burden of most of the air traffic in and out of Berlin. Schönefeld, the former GDR's main international airport and located on the city's southern fringe, is much smaller than Tegel and falls short of western standards. It handled 2.5 million passengers in 1990, and work is under way on increasing capacity to 6 million by the end of 1992.

Currently under discussion is an international airport outside Berlin. The cost, however, would probably exceed DM 12 billion and it would take at least 15 years to build. In the meantime or as an alternative, Schönefeld could easily be expanded due to its location. There are also plans to make Schönefeld into the airport for long-distance international flights, while Tegel serves as the main base for inner-German and European commuter traffic.

The other eastern German airports are small and primitive; all are planning to upgrade. **Leipzig** is expected to count 800,000 passengers this year (expected freight capacity: 5,000 tonnes), compared to 275,000 passengers in 1990. Experts foresee at least 2.4 million passengers annually by 1995. **Dresden** is expected eventually to handle 1.5 million passengers; volume has jumped from 200,000 prior to unification to an estimated 700,000 this year. Currently it has 60 weekly connections to 17 European cities. The eastern German airports are still under Treuhandanstalt management but are in the process of being privatized.

Lufthansa Airport Express

This train service links Frankfurt airport to Düsseldorf (city and airport) via Bonn and Cologne (cities) and to Stuttgart (city). Only passengers holding a valid IATA flight ticket may take the Airport Express for a connecting flight to or from Frankfurt (for example, a passenger with an IATA ticket from Stuttgart to Hong Kong via Frankfurt could choose to take the Airport Express to Frankfurt rather than fly). The Airport Express provides Business Class service, meals and drinks, and the trains commute four times a day in each direction. Travel time between Frankfurt and Düsseldorf: three hours; between Frankfurt and Cologne: one hour and 40 minutes; between Frankfurt and Stuttgart: one and a half hours.

Train Service

The Deutsche Bundesbahn (DB) provides excellent rail connections throughout the country, and train travel is highly recommendable these days given the overcrowded skies and resulting air traffic delays. The Deutsche Reichsbahn (DR), the eastern German railway system, is still in business. Under the motto "Two Railways – One Product" both railways are separate companies for the time being but with integrated schedules and special offers. Due to the lack of private cars in the GDR, emphasis was put on the railway system. Track density is higher than in the west and whereas about 80% of western Germans preferred to travel by car, 66% of eastern Germans relied (or rather: had to rely) on trains.

One of the most positive developments in the cooperation so far has been the eastward expansion of the fast Intercity (IC) train network. ICs not only connect western cities but also commute between Hamburg and Berlin, and between Leipzig and Frankfurt. Until 2 June 1991 these were Germany's fastest and most comfortable trains; 340 of them link 60 cities throughout the country at one-hour intervals from early morning to night. The five main IC lines meet at Cologne, Mannheim, Frankfurt and Würzburg; in case of delay, the trains wait for each other for up to 15 minutes. IC trains have first and second class and charge a DM 6 supplement over the standard fare. Dining cars are very pleasant; coin-operated telephones in the first class section are available to all passengers.

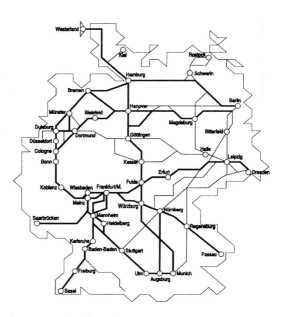

Since 2 June 1991, the new DB baby and "supertrain" is the Intercity Express (ICE). It connects Hamburg and Munich via Kassel, Frankfurt, Mannheim and Stuttgart every hour and travels between 250 and 280 km/h. Starting in the fall, the ICE will debut on a second route, from Hamburg to Munich via Nuremberg. In 1993, a third ICE track is supposed to open from Hamburg to Basel (Switzerland) via Frankfurt and Mannheim. By then, 60 streamlined, high-tech trains will be offering travellers telephones, faxes, fully equipped offices, video in two of the 13 cars and 40-seat restaurants.

Other train categories include the D-trains and Inter Regios, both with first and second class; these trains connect the five main IC routes with numerous smaller cities throughout Germany.

For business people travelling relatively short distances, the ICE and the IC systems are very practical and convenient. From downtown locations it is always quicker to get to the main railway station (traditionally in the centre of the city) than to the nearest airport; many of the ICE and IC train carriages are easy to work in because they are laid out as an aircraft, each seat with a table, two seats abreast and an aisle down the middle (these "Großraumwagen" should be specifically requested when making an advance IC reservation because old-style carriages with six-seater compartments still exist).

Driving

Drivers in the Federal Republic must be in possession of a valid national or international driving licence. A national licence is sufficient for a period of one year for all visitors, an international driving licence is needed for those whose licences Germans cannot read (it is advisable to check with a German embassy or consulate in cases of doubt; for questions regarding a driving licence or car registration once in Germany, ask at the local office of the main German automobile club, ADAC). Car registration papers must be carried at all times; visitors bringing in cars from countries outside the EC should also have an international motor vehicle certificate.

There are a great many dos and don'ts for motorists in Germany. Germans tend to be fast and aggressive drivers who often put their egos behind the wheel. Speed limits such as there are (e.g. 100 km/h on regular two-lane highways) mean very little and the famed German *Autobahns* (motorways with an ignored "recommended" limit of 130 km/h) provide amateur racing drivers with ample practice ground.

In cities, the streets are often so jammed that it is hardly possible to exceed the 50 km/h limit. A recent study showed that German drivers spend an average of 65 hours a year in front of red lights and inner-city traffic jams. Some drivers take off with a screech and stop abruptly. The cities (and *Autobahns* as well) are suffocating from the high number of cars; in the last 30 years, car registrations have increased from 8 to 36 million (and the market in eastern Germany is by no means saturated). Frankfurt alone, a city of 600,000 inhabitants, numbers 190,000 car commuters daily. Bicyclists are a nuisance (from the driver's point of view) and tend to be ignored.

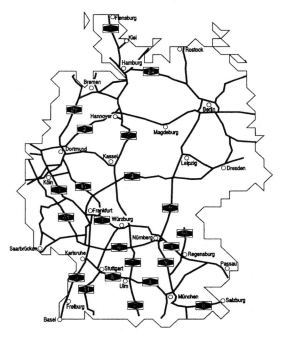

The extensive *Autobahn* network also stretches

into the new states. The West German government used to pay huge sums for permission to build and maintain motorways leading into West Berlin from West Germany. These highways are in relatively good shape. All other highways, streets and roads are not; driving is a bumpy business.

Most *Autobahns* are overcrowded; the best time to travel is probably between 2 and 4 a.m. on a spring or autumn night under perfect weather conditions and a full moon. Quite a number of *Autobahns* still have only two lanes each way and whenever there are road-works or accidents, traffic piles up. Local radio stations (the frequencies are given along the *Autobahn*) give regular traffic advisories, and visitors with a sufficient command of German are recommended to tune in, and if necessary take alternative routes.

Autobahns are heavily used by trucks. Already more than 100,000 German trucks and 25,000 from foreign countries transport their goods on the *Autobahns* and these figures are expected to rise dramatically with the Single European Market in 1993. Only trucks with special permission are allowed to use the *Autobahns* at the weekend.

The main trunk or "B" roads (for Bundesstraße) are generally very good in western Germany. Seat belts on front and rear seats are mandatory; children under 12 may not sit in the front. Cars must be equipped at all times with a warning triangle for emergencies, as well as a first aid kit and rubber gloves. The left lane on the *Autobahn* is for overtaking only and overtaking on the right is strictly forbidden. Emergency phones are at regular intervals along the *Autobahn,* and arrows every 500 metres point to the nearest phone. Generally speaking, and when in doubt, traffic coming from the right has right of way.

Car Rental

All the major car rental agencies are present in the Federal Republic in full force, at all the large airports (also in the new states), most of the small ones, and in all the cities and towns in the west and the bigger cities in the east. To rent a car, a valid driving licence, credit card and a passport are usually required.

Each local office has its own telephone number, but to reserve a car, a local-charge number can be dialled from anywhere in the country (also from the east, although telephone connections are hard to get):

Avis: 01 30/77 33
Hertz: 01 30/21 21
InterRent/Europcar: 01 30/22 11
Sixt Budget: 01 30/33 66

(For travel within cities, see Cities, pages 32-33)

An Overview of the German Economy

Industry and Agriculture

After near stagnation or sluggish growth through much of the past decade, the German economy surged forward again in the period 1988-90. This growth spurt – featuring real year-to-year GNP expansion of 4.6% in 1990 after 3.9% in 1989 and 3.7% in 1988 – drew additional momentum from the opening of Eastern Europe and, in particular, from the merger with East Germany in 1990. Two other important factors were rising volumes of world trade and the increasing degree of economic integration in the European Community.

Although most of western Germany's key manufacturing industries began to reach the limits of their production capacity during the growth spurt starting in 1989, a restrictive monetary policy and an appreciating D-Mark kept inflation in check at just under 3% in 1990. Rising domestic business investment – it was growing at an annual rate of 13% in early 1991 – appears to ensure a sustained expansion of the economy during the first half of the current decade. Rising real personal income was offset in the late Eighties by even stronger gains in labour productivity. Germany remains among the richest countries in the world in terms of per capita GNP.

Unemployment, which had been a chronic structural problem for western Germany throughout most of the past decade, dwindled to under 7% there by the end of 1990, thanks to strong job creation. In eastern Germany, where unemployment had been close to zero before unification, spiralling unemployment resulted from the closing of uneconomical industries. The loss of Comecon markets and the competitive shock of the newly introduced market economy caused production to contract by about one-third in the region in the first year of currency union with western Germany. The mid-1990 currency union gave eastern Germany both buying power and access to western goods. This touched off a wave of pent-up consumerism, which has primarily benefited the economy of western Germany and its chief Western European trading partners.

Transfer payments from western Germany are being used to cushion hardships caused by the economic upheaval in the eastern states. A programme has been launched to rebuild or modernize the neglected communications and transportation infrastructure of eastern Germany in an effort to attract the western business investment needed to revive the regional economy. Government leaders have promised that the standard of living of eastern Germany will catch up with that of the western states by the middle of the current decade. Critics worry, however, that the prosperity gap between the two regions could widen and calcify, leading to social and political instability and depopulation of the east.

The German economy is by far the largest in Europe, excluding the Soviet Union. In 1990, the GNP of western Germany alone amounted to DM 2,448 billion. To this must be added the production of eastern Germany, estimated in 1989, the last full year before currency union and unification, at DM 286 billion, or between 10% and 15% of that the west. Although eastern German production fell sharply thereafter, western Germany's grew strongly. Thus the combined German economy at current prices and exchange rates in 1990 was about double the size of that of the UK. It was also at least a third larger than that of France, half as large as Japan's and a quarter as large as that of the US.

Germany is poor in natural resources and too densely settled for large-scale agriculture, which accounts for under 4% of production. Nevertheless, over 35% of all land is now used for agriculture or is under permanent cultivation (this compares with 30% in the Federal Republic before unification). In Sachsen-Anhalt and Mecklenburg-Vorpommern, the proportion exceeds 50%. Germany produces over one-fifth of total EC grain and 38% of the EC potato harvest.

The country's economy has also been slower than that of the US or the UK in the shift to services, which account for only around 57% of GNP in the west and perhaps half that level in the east. The main thrust of the German economy remains manufacturing, which together with mining accounts for 41% of GNP in the west and two-thirds of it in the east. Leading German industries include automobiles, machinery and plant engineering, chemicals and electrical engineering. Capital goods production, particularly for export, is a longtime German strength.

Of all the large industrial countries, Germany has the most open economy as illustrated by the high ratio of foreign trade to total output. For western Germany alone, foreign trade in 1990 totalled DM 1,193 billion. Until unification, Germany had consistently produced more than it consumed. Then the booming economy in the western states and the wave of pent-up consumerism from the eastern states turned the tables. With western German industry producing at full capacity, the country began to draw in ever larger amounts of imports to satisfy domestic demand, the economy's new engine. As a result, Germany's trade and current account surpluses shrank rapidly at the start of the Nineties with signs that they will swing into deficits.

This radical shift in Germany's international balance of payments could have profound consequences beyond the country's borders. Leading German trading partners are finding it easier to redress their trade deficits with Germany. Moreover, the potential German capital account surplus which would inevitably accompany a current account deficit would eventually convert Germany into a net international borrower. This capital inflow would place further strain on the overburdened international capital markets.

The costs of unification and reconstruction of eastern Germany will obviously be huge. But western Germany has begun this process from a sound fiscal and monetary position. Its ratio of private financial savings was among the highest in the world at about 14% in 1990. With some DM 3.1 trillion in accumulated financial savings of various types, Germans could in theory afford to finance unification out of pocket. Nevertheless, the effort will take its toll on the country's high standard of living.

The government initially attempted to shift this burden to future generations by raising the necessary funds through capital market borrowing. The result was that the ratio of public deficits to GNP was expected to double from the healthy 1989 level of around 4%. This dangerous development was offset in 1991 by the imposition of new taxes, which have a more immediate impact on the level of prosperity.

The Bundesbank is expected to maintain its tight monetary policy to offset the inflationary impact of the government's expansionary fiscal policy. German industry, which is in possession of high levels of liquidity, has shifted much of its investment activity from the European Community to the new eastern states since currency union.

Foreign Trade

In 1990, Germany recovered its title as the world's leading exporter after having been ousted briefly from this position by the US in 1989. Adding in data for the new eastern states for the period following the mid-1990 currency union, Germany in 1990 exported goods worth DM 662 billion and imported wares for DM 557 billion, leaving a German merchandise trade surplus of just over DM 105 billion. Ignoring its trade with eastern Germany, western Germany alone notched a merchandise trade surplus of DM 92 billion for 1990, exporting goods worth DM 643 billion and importing DM 551 billion worth.

Some 53% of German foreign trade in 1990 was with other European Community members, with France leading the group. Including EFTA countries, Germany does 71% of its foreign trade with Western Europe. The share of German trade with all the industrialized countries combined, including the US, Japan and Canada, just exceeds 84%. That leaves less than 16% of the country's total trade to be divided up between developing countries, OPEC nations and Eastern Europe.

Unification has resulted in a dramatic swing in the German balance of payments. This was illustrated by the contraction of the western German trade surplus to DM 92 billion from DM 135 billion in 1989. While exports were up only slightly, imports jumped by around 8%. The country's current account surplus shrank, meanwhile, to around DM 72 billion on a partly combined basis in 1990 from a record DM 104 billion for West Germany in 1989. The trend continued in early 1991 and some banking analysts predicted Germany would be showing a current account deficit as early as the full year 1992.

The development of the German economy has been deeply divided since unification. While western Germany is enjoying strong growth, production in eastern Germany is plunging. Pervasive underemployment (unemployment and short-time work) is the most striking social problem posed by structural change in the east. The uncertain outlook on the labour market is bearing down heavily on large sections of the population. At the same time, high transfer payments to ease the social costs have cut deep into the federal budget; the impending tax increases are intended to plug this drain on resources. But despite all the difficulties, indications of a turnaround are mounting: 1992 will see the start of an economic upswing in eastern Germany.

Growth of Gross National Product (% change)

e = estimate; f = forecast

Eastern Germany

Growth/business climate. The crisis triggered by the economic and social upheaval in the east is not yet over; industrial production has still not bottomed out. In the first quarter of 1991, industrial production was about 50% lower than in the year-earlier period. After sliding roughly 17% in 1990, real GNP looks set to shrivel another 17% despite massive injections of funds from the west.

The various state business promotion schemes have yet to yield something greater than the sum of their parts. Capital spending and production at many companies is being hampered by a wide range of problems. These include questions of ownership and valuation, the unresolved matter of who should assume old debts, inadequate infrastructure, the overburdened administration including the Treuhandanstalt, low productivity and overstaffing at existing large companies. The time needed to adjust after the switch from socialism to capitalism was underestimated by many, including the federal government. Consequently, the government had to boost its financial support in the first quarter of 1991.

The Sachverständigenrat, the German council of economic advisors, did however issue a timely warning in March 1991 against doing too much of the wrong thing. This admonition was directed at the economic firemen who are restricting their efforts to extinguishing fires already burning. What is needed, however, is a new structure that prevents fires (read: state intervention) from starting in the first place. The federal government has yet to put forward a convincing strategy on this score. But what about the economic upswing to come? Positive indications will multiply in the second half of this year, and the upturn will begin in 1992, with 12% growth forecasted. What must not be overlooked is the very low starting point. The main sources of hope and growth are the construction business and certain service sectors such as banking and transport, where there are already clear signs of improvement.

Overall capital investment should pick up as early as the second half of 1991. A good DM 40 billion has been earmarked this year for government transfer payments to promote capital investment. Investment by western German companies is also fast accelerating: according to an extensive new survey by the Ifo economic research institute, western German companies plan to increase capital spending in eastern Germany to DM 13.5 billion in 1991, compared with DM 4.2 billion in the previous year (see table). For 1992 a further climb to DM 19 billion is envisaged. After service industries – especially banking – led the way in capital spending last year, the manufacturing industries are now moving to the fore.

The stumbling block for large-scale capital spending by eastern German companies remains the shortage of capital. Consequently, as with the West German economic miracle of the Fifties and Sixties, small companies will have to act as the driving force

Capital Spending and Capital Investment Plans of Western German Companies in Eastern Germany from 1990 to 1992 (according to Ifo survey, in DM billion)

	1990	1991	1992
Manufacturing	2.0	10.0	15.0
Construction	0.2	0.6	0.6
Trading	0.7	1.3	1.4
Banking	1.0	1.1	1.4
Insurance	0.3	0.5	0.6
Total	4.2	13.5	19.0

Source: Ifo special survey, November 1990 to February 1991

behind the economy. A total of 254,400 new companies (balance of new companies registered and existing companies closed down) were recorded in 1990, of which roughly 60% are estimated actually to have opened for business. The growth trend is continuing in 1991. Nearly half of these new businesses are in the trading, hotel or restaurant sectors, followed by skilled crafts with a good 10% share. The free-lance professions still have a lot of ground to make up. Measured by western German standards, about 100,000 self-employed people are needed in medicine, the legal profession and business and tax consultancy; but in February 1991, eastern Germany had only 18,000 professionals active in these fields.

The massive support from western Germany appears to be virtually a guarantee of economic growth in 1992. But what is crucial for further economic development in eastern Germany is that a lasting self-sustaining recovery sets in. Whether this happens remains an open question.

Wage increases in eastern Germany, largely the result of social policy considerations, but highly inadvisable in economic terms, are giving cause for concern. The trend is inadvisable because it has been completely divorced from productivity. Real wages first rose dramatically owing to the conversion to the D-Mark, and then as a result of massive wage increases. In many

Assessment of Capital Investment Conditions in Eastern Germany by Western German Manufacturing Companies

(Percentage of respondents citing each factor)

Advantages (incentives)

Market proximity for business in eastern Germany	82
Bridgehead to Eastern Europe	45
Capacity limits reached in western Germany	25
Skilled labour	21
Favourable capital investment and financing conditions	12
Lower wage costs than in western Germany	11
Return to old location	5
Other	5

Disadvantages (disincentives)

Valuation questions	36
Infrastructure weaknesses	32
Uncertain situation regarding clean-up of contaminated sites	27
Legal problems with purchase of land	24
Uncertain market development in Eastern Europe	18
Delays in authorization of operations or building	15
Wage costs	12
Financing	9
Other	6

Source: Ifo special survey, November 1990 to February 1991

sectors, wage hikes to 50 to 60% of western German levels have already been agreed for 1991, while eastern German productivity in the manufacturing sector is less than 30% of that of western Germany. The average wage in eastern Germany had reached DM 1,500 by October 1990, and is now three times higher than the average in Poland. High wages are counter-productive for employment, as they either completely deter many investors or they encourage them to invest in capital-intensive labour-saving operations. The deterrent effect chiefly applies to foreign investors.

Eastern Germany: Unemployment and Short-Time Work (in millions)

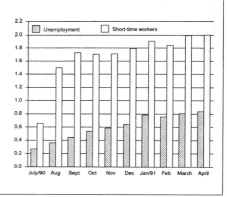

For western German companies, the common language and administration compensate for high wage costs compared with those in other Eastern European states undertaking reforms.

In April 1991, 836,941 unemployed and 2 million short-time workers were registered in eastern Germany. The latter figure conceals high additional unemployment, as average employment of short-time workers in April was only about 40%. We expect unemployment to peak in early 1992, with approximately 1.3 million unemployed and over 2 million short-time workers. This takes into account the extensive efforts by the government to reduce the official extent of underemployment through generous provisions for early retirement and training courses (job-creation schemes). The number of people in employment is likely to drop from 9.5 million in 1989 to 5.5 million in the coming year.

Nonetheless, economic policy-makers should avoid delaying the necessary structural change by using state intervention in the guise of excessive subsidies to prop up businesses and maintain jobs. Otherwise, the eastern German economy runs the risk, under the cover of restructuring, of becoming permanently dependent on state subsidies.

The situation is much the same regarding the introduction of market prices. Many prices have successively been deregulated in eastern Germany since early 1991. This sent the annualized inflation rate for January soaring to 7.4%, after average consumer prices in 1990 had consistently remained under the year-earlier level. But the decision to defer the adjustment of rents was a step backward, which for the time being is having a detrimental effect on private housing construction.

Another factor delaying the desired economic upturn is the impact of forty years of socialism on the eastern German work ethic. Some western companies feel that eastern German employees lack a sense of initiative and are unwilling or afraid to take on responsibility. These problems will, however, in the course of time disappear of their own accord.

At present around 60% of eastern German income is drawn from western German social transfer payments and only about 40% from production in the new *Länder*. This has prompted many warnings on the perils of a subsidy mentality taking root. For some individuals and certain areas of the economy this is probable, but for the vast majority of the population, their own self-esteem will prevent this happening.

Living standard/real income. The average eastern German living standard has improved appreciably since the introduction of currency, economic and social union and the country's subsequent incorporation into the Federal Republic. The clear winners in material terms are those in secure employment. The increase in their income has more than offset the loss from the deregulation of previously fixed prices. The real purchasing power of pensioners is also climbing. But there are, at least for the time being, also losers – contrary to the extravagant assertions made by politicians in the run-up to the December 1990 election. Their ranks include the majority of the unemployed and some of the short-time workers, though the comprehensive social security payments have saved them from undue financial hardship. The high wage increases agreed mean that income differentials in real terms will in future broaden markedly.

Comparison of reforms in eastern Germany and other Eastern European countries. From an eastern German perspective, the frequent demands for a rapid wage convergence with western Germany are understandable. The aim in the iron and steel industry is to attain this target by 1994. In this rush up the income ladder, it is easy to forget how the eastern German standard of living compares with that of their former partners elsewhere in Eastern Europe. The gap in living standard between eastern Germany and Poland, Czechoslovakia and Hungary, the leaders of the reform movement in Eastern Europe, has widened drastically in favour of eastern Germany. Thanks to extensive western German support for the build-up of an internationally competitive infrastructure and administration, the discrepancy in per capita income will widen even further. Eastern Germany will soon match Spain and presumably, within a few years, the UK. For the other Eastern European states en route to reform, development along the lines of that in Portugal would be quite welcome.

Placing a figure on government transfers from western to eastern Germany clarifies the situation: including Gemeinschaftswerk Aufschwung Ost, a government initiative to promote recovery in the east, and the German Unity Fund, payments for 1991 will come to DM 140 billion. This amounts to DM 8,500 (about $5,000) for each eastern German. This figure alone is far higher than per capita income in Poland (1990: $2,100), Czechoslovakia ($3,000) and Hungary ($3,200).

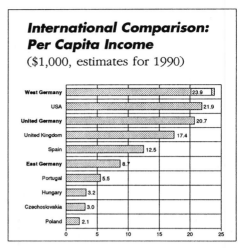

International Comparison: Per Capita Income
($1,000, estimates for 1990)

Western Germany

Growth/business activity. With the political change in the former GDR, the western German economy began to break out of the business cycle prevalent in other western industrial nations (see chart below). Whereas the US and the UK in particular slid into recession during 1990, western Germany recorded a 4.5% increase in real GNP, the highest growth rate since 1976. A major reason for this boom was the extreme surge in demand from eastern Germany in connection with an expansive fiscal policy. Domestic private demand had already received a boost in early 1990 from tax cuts.

In 1991 circumstances are changing, and real GNP growth will, in our view, contract to 3.0%. Demand from the new *Länder*, fuelled by extensive transfer payments, is still high, but the initial surge has now petered out. The development of the economy is being dampened by the decline in exports because of the recession in the western industrial nations and will receive a further blow when increases in tax and social security payments take effect on 1 July 1991. The effect of this will be to slash private purcha-

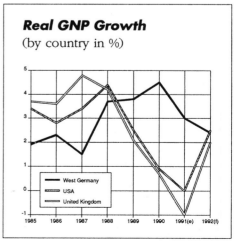

Real GNP Growth
(by country in %)

sing power by DM 50 billion in the first twelve months. On the other hand, capital spending will prop up growth this year and next. Despite this slight downturn, Japan is the only one of the major industrial nations which will achieve higher growth than western Germany in 1991.

After a period of slower growth in the first half the western German economy will pick up again in the second half of 1992, with the capital goods industry being fed by the incipient upswing in the new *Länder*. The outlook for exports is improving as western countries draw out of the recession, the D-Mark depreciates in real terms, and business activity surges once more before the completion of the Single European Market.

Unification unhitched western Germany from the normal business cycle; 1992 will mark a decade of uninterrupted growth. The build-up of eastern Germany means that subsequent years will also be characterized by special developments. Germany seems unlikely to move back in step with the world economy until the second half of the Nineties.

Employment/wage trends. Strong economic growth caused the number of employed to climb a good 1 million over the last two years to 28.4 million. Despite the influx of workers from the east and the growing number of eastern Germans living in the east and working in the west, average unemployment sank from 2.24 million in 1988 to 1.88 million in 1990. This year the figure will fall to approximately 1.65 million. In 1992 growth in employment will slow down owing to above-average wage increases and as a lagging indicator of weaker economic growth. Estimates made by the economic research body Institut der Deutschen Wirtschaft put western German labour costs at DM 37.9 per hour in 1990 (manufacturing industry, including incremental staff costs), substantially higher than anywhere else in the world. Regardless of this, nominal wage increases reached through collective bargaining in 1991 are, at 6-7%, slightly higher than in previous years.

Inflation. A high degree of price stability is the principal stated objective of the Bundesbank. Its policy has always been a success in past years: on average, western German consumer prices climbed only 2.7% in 1990, al-

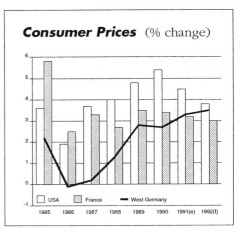

Consumer Prices (% change)

USA ☐ France ▨ West Germany ▬

1985 1986 1987 1988 1989 1990 1991(e) 1992(f)

though German economic union and then rising oil prices had aroused fears of markedly higher inflation. In the first four months of 1991 the annual inflation rate remained at an average 2.7%. A steeper increase is expected for the second half of the year owing to consumer tax increases slated for 1 July, high wage rises and increased import prices as a result of the depreciation of the D-Mark. To keep down inflation, the Bundesbank has consistently opposed a reduction in key interest rates. At times there has been massive pressure from the US, the UK and France for a reduction in German interest rates to stimulate the world economy. We estimate that the western German inflation rate will climb to an average 3.4% for 1991.

Federal budget. The extremely high costs of unification came at a financially favourable time for the Federal Republic. In 1989 there was a slight budget surplus and tax revenue was profiting from the boom in western Germany. The costs of adopting the market economy in eastern Germany were, however, underestimated. The high government transfer payments led to a budget deficit in 1990 of 2.0% of GNP. In 1991, transfer payments are making even deeper inroads into government spending. With further pressure from the share in financing the Gulf War, the deficit will rise to roughly 5.0% of GNP, which is significantly higher than the much-discussed US deficit (see chart at right). This estimate takes into account the additional revenue from increases in tax and social security contributions. After the government even promised in autumn 1990, before the federal elections, to avoid tax increases, unexpectedly high increases were passed in March 1991. The greatest increases in revenue will come from raising income tax and mineral oil tax.

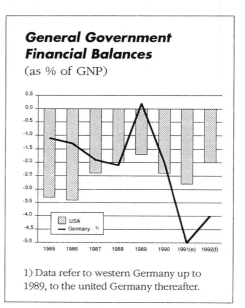

General Government Financial Balances
(as % of GNP)

1) Data refer to western Germany up to 1989, to the united Germany thereafter.

Interest rate trends. Interest rates have now passed their peak in Germany as well. After climbing noticeably since mid-1989, the government bond yield reached its high of a good 9% in the last quarter of 1990. Following the Gulf War, it slipped to 8.5%. For the time being a further fall is being prevented by the restrictive monetary policy of the Bundesbank and the high demand for capital in eastern Germany. As international interest rates continue to sink, there should be scope for cutting the German government bond yield to 8.2% in early 1992.

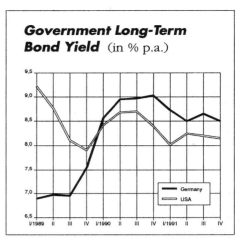

Government Long-Term Bond Yield (in % p.a.)

Exchange rates. From mid-February to early-May 1991 the value of the D-Mark fell from DM 1.45 to DM 1.75 per dollar. During this period the renewed strength of the dollar (increased international confidence and enhanced geopolitical status following success in the Gulf War, expectations of an imminent economic recovery) coincided with the weakness of the D-Mark (economic crisis in eastern Germany, proximity to the politically and economically unstable Soviet Union). Part of the change in the exchange rate is, however, due to the previous excessive devaluation of the dollar.

By the end of the year we expect the dollar to climb to DM 1.85, as

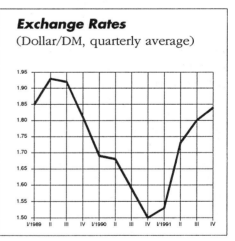

Exchange Rates
(Dollar/DM, quarterly average)

the leading economic indicators (inflation, business activity) will develop in favour of the US and the interest rate differential will not widen any further. The pressure for devaluation of the D-Mark will ease when there are clear signs of a recovery in eastern Germany. We expect this development to take place in 1992.

Foreign trade/balance of payments. German foreign trade is also clearly feeling the effect of unification. The surge in demand from eastern Germany and the ensuing boom in western Germany pushed imports of goods up to a higher level than usual. Their value climbed 9.9% to DM 556.6 billion. At the same time, export growth slowed owing to the recession in the other western industrial nations, which are the main buyers of German exports. The value of goods exported rose just under 3.3% to DM 661.9 billion. Consequently, the German trade surplus sank from DM 135 billion in the previous year to DM 105 billion.

This development is much more marked in 1991. Weak export activity, chiefly stemming from the worldwide recession, is being exacerbated by the collapse of eastern German exports to former Comecon countries. In April Germany recorded its first monthly trade deficit since August 1981. For 1991 in total, the trade balance will remain in surplus, but the amount will contract drastically to less than DM 10 billion, according to our estimates. In the coming year this trend will come to a halt. Owing to the upturn in the world economy and the typical delayed impact of depreciation of the D-Mark, German export business will pick up again.

With regard to the current account, the reduction of the foreign trade imbalance will be even more pronounced in 1991. With the surplus having already sunk in 1990 by DM 30 billion to DM 77.4 billion, the German current account will show its first deficit since 1981. For the first four months of 1991 the deficit amounted to DM 12 billion, just partly due to Germany's contribution to financing the Gulf War.

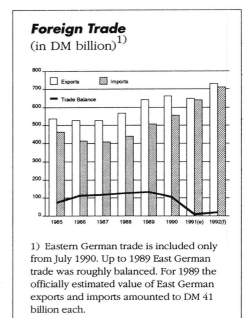

Foreign Trade
(in DM billion)[1]

1) Eastern German trade is included only from July 1990. Up to 1989 East German trade was roughly balanced. For 1989 the officially estimated value of East German exports and imports amounted to DM 41 billion each.

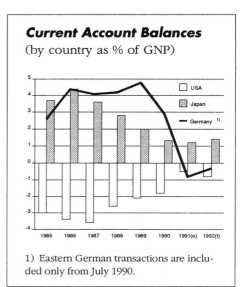

Current Account Balances
(by country as % of GNP)

1) Eastern German transactions are included only from July 1990.

Germany: Economic Profile and Forecast

			1990	1991 (e)	1992 (f)
1 United Germany					
Gross National Product	(GNP; DM bn)	1)	2,658	2,796	2,990
Real GNP growth	(%)	1)	2.7	1.5	3.1
GNP per capita	(DM)	1)	33,595	35,056	37,095
GNP per capita	(US $)	1)	20,737	20,263	19,943
Exports	(fob; DM bn)	2)	661.9	648.7	730.5
Imports	(cif; DM bn)	2)	556.6	640.1	710.5
Trade balance	(DM bn)	2)	105.3	8.6	20.0
Current account balance	(DM bn)	2)	77.4	-22.0	-10.0
Government finance	(balance in % of GNP)		-2.0	-5.0	-4.0
Government bond yield	(% p.a.; annual average)		8.9	8.6	8.2
Exchange rate DM/US $	(annual average)		1.62	1.73	1.86
Exchange rate DM/US $	(year-end)		1.49	1.85	1.82
2 Western Germany					
Gross National Product	(GNP; DM bn)		2,426	2,584	2,738
Real GNP growth	(%)		4.5	3.0	2.4
GNP per capita	(DM)		38,742	40,852	42,720
GNP per capita	(US $)		23,915	23,614	22,968
Inflation	(annual average; %)		2.7	3.4	3.5
Employment	(000s, annual average)		28,440	29,100	29,600
Unemployment	(000s, annual average)		1,883	1,650	1,550
Rate of unemployment	(%, annual average)		6.4	5.6	5.2
3 Eastern Germany					
Gross National Product	(GNP; DM bn)	3)	232	212	251
Real GNP growth	(%)		-17.0	-17.0	12.0
GNP per capita	(DM)		14,061	12,837	15,240
GNP per capita	(US $)		8,679	7,420	8,195
Unemployment	(000s, year-end)		642	1,300	1,150
Rate of unemployment	(%, year-end)		7.3	15.0	13.0
Workers on short hours	(000s, year-end)		1,794	2,200	1,900

(e): Estimate
(f): Forecast
1) Figures for 1990 are based on estimates for the East German share.
2) Up to June 1990 these figures are for West Germany only.
3) Rough estimate for 1990; official figure available only for second half of 1990 (DM 105.3 bn).

Sources: Statistisches Bundesamt, Deutsche Bundesbank, OECD, estimates and forecasts by F.A.Z. GmbH Information Services.

Volker Sach

Tops in Germany

Top 100 Companies

	Group turnover in DM million	Employees
1. Daimler-Benz	85500	376,785
2. Volkswagen AG	68061	261,000
3. Siemens AG	63185	408,000
4. Mercedes-Benz Aktiengesellschaft	59800	231,000
5. Veba Aktiengesellschaft	54600	106,900
6. BASF Aktiengesellschaft	46623	134,647
7. Hoechst Aktiengesellschaft	44862	172,890
8. RWE Aktiengesellschaft	44235	97,596
9. Tengelmann Group	42218	165,000
10. Bayer Aktiengesellschaft	41643	170,200
11. Thyssen Aktiengesellschaft	36185	152,078
12. Rewe Handelsgruppe	32208	120,000
13. Robert Bosch GmbH	31800	181,000
14. BMW Aktiengesellschaft	27177	70,948
15. Mannesmann AG	24000	124,000
16. Deutsche Bundesbahn	23770	232,400
17. Opel Aktiengesellschaft	23707	57,489
18. Ruhrkohle Aktiengesellschaft	22921	124,838
19. Deutsche Bundespost Postdienst	22000	390,000
20. Edeka Zentrale AG	22000	700
21. ALDI Group	21500*	20,000
22. REWE & Co. oHG	21090	64,639
23. Metallgesellschaft Aktiengesellschaft	19827	32,224
24. Ford-Werke Aktiengesellschaft	19806	50,121

	Group turnover in DM million	Employees
25. Viag Aktiengesellschaft	19479	55,797
26. Preussag Aktiengesellschaft	19046	72,500
27. MAN Aktiengesellschaft	18900	66,000
28. RWE-DEA AG	17828	5,430
29. Stinnes AG	17600	21,238
30. Veba Oel AG	17292	21,480
31. Karstadt Aktiengesellschaft	16768	66,000
32. Fried. Krupp GmbH	15800	58,900
33. Franz Haniel & Cie. GmbH	15000 +	24,000
34. Kaufhof Holding Aktiengesellschaft	14692	46,700
35. Deutsche Lufthansa Aktiengesellschaft	14447	57,567
36. Otto Versand Handelsgruppe	14358	32,081
37. Degussa AG	13925	35,005
38. Esso AG	13628 *	2,000
39. IBM Deutschland GmbH	13324	31,767
40. Bertelsmann AG	13313	45,000
41. AEG Aktiengesellschaft	13100	76,900
42. Deutsche BP Aktiengesellschaft	12810 +	5,521
43. Deutsche Shell Aktiengesellschaft	12800	3,254
44. Thyssen Handelsunion AG	12777	24,322
45. Hoesch AG	12570	53,000
46. Quelle Gruppe	12570	39,300
47. Deutsche Aerospace AG	12525	63,000
48. Audi AG	12125	37,914
49. Henkel KGaA	12017	38,803
50. Aral Aktiengesellschaft	11581 *	899
51. Gedelfi GmbH + Co. KG	11026	144
52. Asko Deutsche Kaufhaus AG	10559 *	34,456
53. Metro Gruppe Deutschland	10846 *	13,000
54. Hüls Aktiengesellschaft	10206	20,898
55. Klöckner & Co. Aktiengesellschaft	9854	8,274
56. Thyssen Stahl Aktiengesellschaft	9734	41,253
57. Feldmühle Nobel Aktiengesellschaft	9408 +	32,044
58. Philipp Holzmann Aktiengesellschaft	9188	36,830
59. PreussenElektra Aktiengesellschaft	9099	17,245

	Group turnover in DM million	Employees
60. Deutsche Unilever GmbH	8969	25,259
61. Ruhrgas Aktiengesellschaft	8841 *	2,933
62. Toepfer International	8782	752
63. Philips GmbH	8740	30,000
64. Continental AG	8550	51,100
65. Spar Handels-Aktiengesellschaft	8398	16,457
66. BATIG Gesellschaft für Beteiligungen mbH	8366	23,911
67. Raab Karcher AG	8177	15,322
68. Schenker & Co. GmbH	8060	12,781
69. Thyssen Industrie AG	7907	48,581
70. Krupp Stahl AG	7872	25,147
71. AGIV Aktiengesellschaft	7500	47
72. Klöckner-Werke AG	7487	35,000
73. C. & A. Brenninkmeyer KG	7375 *	n/a
74. Agfa-Gevaert AG	7100	29,784
75. Tchibo Holding Aktiengesellschaft	6871 *	8,300
76. Wintershall AG	6700	3,200
77. Reemstma GmbH	6676	5,035
78. Asea Brown Boveri Aktiengesellschaft	6649	35,000
79. IFA-Bundeszentrale 6600	55	
80. Schaper Gruppe	6522	18,223
81. Bosch-Siemens Hausgeräte GmbH	6498	23,000
82. Aachener und Münchener Beteiligungs-AG	6441 *	8,924
83. Philip Morris GmbH	6399 *	4,000
84. Vereinigte Elektrizitätswerke Westfalen AG	6330	8,075
85. Allfonds Gesellschaft für Investmentanlagen mbH	6300	44
86. Stahlwerke Peine-Salzgitter AG	6206	11,282
87. Hertie Waren- und Kaufhaus GmbH	6178	34,000
88. Nestlé Deutschland GmbH	6100	14,734
89. Linde Aktiengesellschaft	6069	27,676
90. Bayernwerk	6013	9,570
91. Hochtief Aktiengesellschaft	6000	26,000
92. Schering Aktiengesellschaft	5923	26,695
93. BayWa Aktiengesellschaft München	5734	11,142

	Group turnover in DM million	Employees
94. Vereinigte Aluminium Werke AG	5727	16,323
95. Deutsche Babcock AG	5524	30,000
96. Kühne & Nagel AG & Co.	5520	8,700
97. Lidl & Schwarz Stiftung & Co. KG	5500	15,000
98. MAN Nutzfahrzeuge Aktiengesellschaft	5500	19,836
99. Mobil Oil AG	5497	2,081
100. Kaufring AG	5400	1,440

Top 16 Banks

	Group business volume in DM million	Employees
1. Deutsche Bank Aktiengesellschaft	404700	68,552
2. Dresdner Bank Aktiengesellschaft	286951	42,217
3. Westdeutsche Landesbank Girozentrale	2510000	8,250
4. Commerzbank Aktiengesellschaft	217946	27,631
5. DG BANK Deutsche Genossenschafts-bank	214931	10,748
6. Bayerische Vereinsbank Aktien-gesellschaft	206000	20,195
7. Bayerische Landesbank Girozentrale	166300	4,526
8. Kreditanstalt für Wiederaufbau	137223	954
9. Bayerische Hypotheken- und Wechsel-Bank AG	124481	12,430
10. Hessische Landesbank Girozentrale	88824	2,621
11. Deutsche Girozentrale - Deutsche Kommunalbank	87874	396
12. Südwestdeutsche Landesbank	87500	2,421
13. Norddeutsche Landesbank Girozentrale	81690	5,997
14. Deutsche Pfandbrief- und Hypotheken-bank AG	64822	709
15. Landeskreditbank Baden-Württemberg	60900	1,212
16. Bank für Gemeinwirtschaft	60279	7,981

Top Insurance Companies

	Group premium income in DM million	Employees
1. Allianz Aktiengesellschaft Holding	31800 *	41,750
2. Münchener Rückversicherungs-Gesellschaft	12459	1,780
3. Allianz Versicherungs-Aktiengesellschaft	10400 *	19,585
4. Allianz Lebensversicherungs-AG	8919 *	4,665
5. Iduna/Nova Gruppe	5572	5,992
6. R + V Versicherung Holding AG	5300	8,482
7. Bayerische Versicherungskammer	4340	3,909
8. Vereinte Versicherungen	4240	5,319
9. Volksfürsorge Holding AG	3703 *	7,086
10. Haftpflichtverband der Deutschen Industrie V.a.G.	3642	3,149
11. Debeka Versicherung und Bausparkasse	3581	7,067
12. HUK-Coburg Versicherungsgruppe	3331 *	4,500
13. Hamburg-Mannheimer Versicherungs-AG	3292	10,970
14. Gothaer Gruppe	3185	4,517
15. Deutsche Krankenversicherung AG	3121	5,887
16. Colonia Versicherung AG	2538	4,833

* 1989 figures: 1990 results are not yet available
+ estimated figures
n/a: figures not available

Laura Covill
"Germany's Top 300: Edition 1991"

Germany's Major Industries

Automobiles

The German automobile industry posted record results in 1990. The Automobile Industry Association (VDA) computed western German vehicle production at 4.98 million units in 1990, a 3% increase over the previous peak of 4.85 million, reached in 1989. The highest growth rate was in commercial vehicle production, which climbed 10% in 1990. Car production rose 2% to 4.66 million vehicles. The figures for German cars produced abroad also showed a marked 8% advance. In 1990 a total of 1.8 million German vehicles were manufactured in other countries.

Given that world vehicle production declined by just under 2% in 1990, and that output was down 1% in European countries, the growth in the German automotive industry is all the more remarkable. This development can largely be explained by the domestic situation. VDA reports that domestic sales reached the unprecedented level of 3.04 million units. The reason for this is low market saturation in eastern Germany and the resultant demand for new vehicles in western Germany, where 30% of all vehicles were deregistered in 1990, a previously unheard-of figure. In eastern Germany, VDA estimates that 600,000 used German cars were sold in 1990, 200,000 foreign imports and 70,000 new vehicles.

Like mechanical engineering, the auto industry had a poor year for export business. Exports were 4.4% lower than the record set in 1989. The only segment to make greater inroads abroad was cars of 3 litres capacity and over (+7.2%). Exports of commercial vehicles also declined in 1990; heavy goods vehicles (over 6.6 tonnes total weight) were particularly hard hit, with export sales sinking 17.8%.

Imports of foreign makes in 1990 present a very different picture, with western German market share up 2% to 32.3%. There was above-average 14.8% growth in new registrations of foreign cars, while new registrations of German models increased 4.2%. According to figures from the Federal Office for Motor Traffic, in the first two months of 1991 Italian producers expanded their market share in western Germany to 5.2% and French producers to 8.7%. Japanese makes only reached 11.2%, down from 15.4% in the whole of 1990.

The auto industry did not perform as well in eastern Germany as in western Germany, with production declining 30% in 1990. Western makes are recording the highest sales, and thus the stock of vehicles increased appreciably despite the slump in production: 4.8 million cars were registered at year-end. This corresponds to growth of 23.5% or 900,000 vehicles. The stock of commercial vehicles climbed by just short of 6% to 7,775,000. The VDA therefore calculates vehicle density for eastern Germany at 298 cars per 1,000 inhabitants. Western Germany has 487 vehicles per 1,000 inhabitants, almost 200 higher.

In early 1991, vehicle production was being driven exclusively by domestic demand. In February 1991, car exports fell 27%, yielding an aggregate export slump of 24% for the first two months of the year. A weakening of the domestic boom is also apparent from the order books, according to VDA's figures, although demand remains high. All in all, sharp decreases in exports and sliding domestic demand mean that frequent forecasts of stagnating growth will finally come true in 1991. To what extent production declines depends on the development of exports; domestic demand may fail to balance out the slump in this area.

The Automobile Industry: 1990 in Figures

1. Sales	
– in DM billion	143.0
– % change 89/90	9%
2. Production	
– No. of vehicles, western Germany	4,976,532
– % change 89/90	2.6%
– No. of vehicles, eastern Germany	186,890
– % change 89/90	– 30%
3. Exports	
– No. of vehicles, western Germany	2,765,646
– % change 89/90	– 4.6%
– No. of vehicles, eastern Germany	122,743
4. Exports as % of production	
– Western Germany	55.6%
– Eastern Germany	65.7%
5. Workforce	
– in 1,000	895
– % change 89/90	2%

Source: VDA

Chemicals

For the chemical industry 1990 was the eighth straight year of growth. However, business in the sector has begun to sag and is trailing behind the economy as a whole. This is clear from a glance at production, where the growth rate is below average at 2.3%. There was no mistaking the impact the unfavourable situation in 1990 had on chemical industry earnings, which were down 20% to 30%. Earnings fell 37.3% at BASF and 22.5% at Hoechst, while the drop at the Bayer group was "limited" to 18%. Preliminary estimates indicate that net return on sales in the sector slipped from 4.6% to 3.5%.

There are various reasons for these trends: the revaluation of the D-Mark against the dollar has put pressure on profits and the competitive position of German chemical companies. Demand also weakened in the US, the UK, Spain and Italy, and subsided even further in Eastern Europe. In some business segments, recent capital investment generated excess capacity, which combined with rising unit costs to send sales prices tumbling. Whereas producer prices in the manufacturing sector for 1990 were 1.5% higher than in 1989, prices fell by about the same extent in the chemical industry. The Gulf War burdened the industry with additional cost pressures owing to oil price increases approaching 100%.

Chemicals: 1990 in Figures

1. Sales	
– in DM billion	162.5
– % change 89/90	1.4%
2. Exports	
– in DM billion	84.5
– % change 89/90	– 1.8%
3. Imports	
– in DM billion	53.1
– % change 89/90	3.5%
4. Workforce	
– in 1,000	592.4
– % change 89/90	1.8%

Source: German Chemical Industry Association

The end of the Gulf conflict and the recovery of the dollar are making life easier for the chemical industry. Expectations of 2% growth in production seem realistic. German chemical companies are certainly optimistic about the medium and long-term outlook. This is reflected in capital spending plans for 1991 totalling a good DM 13 billion, though this figure probably includes outlays for environmental protection, a commitment the industry cannot avoid.

Representatives of western German companies and the Treuhandanstalt are taking a positive medium-term view of the eastern German chemical industry. Some adjustments necessary in this area have already been made: of the more than 100,000 eastern Germans formerly employed in the largest state-owned combines (Bitterfeld, Wolfen, Leuna, Buna and Piesteritz), 30,000 have already been made redundant.

The Treuhandanstalt assumes that about 35,000 workers will be kept on in the end. In some cases it is already certain that the old locations can be used in future. Moreover, some enterprises are being privatized, but others are either too obsolete or too environmentally hazardous to continue operating. Consequently, about 100 operations in the coal-based chemicals industry had already been closed down by the end of 1990.

Construction

The construction industry had another successful year in 1990. The industry's umbrella organization reports that construction turnover came to DM 139.67 billion, a good 12% gain on 1989. The production index was up 4.8% on the previous year (calculated per working day) and the number of people employed in the industry increased 3.7% to 1,033,600.

The driving force behind this vigorous business activity was housing construction. In this area, new orders in 1990 were 17.7% higher in real terms than in the previous year, compared with 8.8% for commercial construction and 3.3% for the public sector.

At the beginning of 1991, construction demand dipped for the first time in 38 months: the order volume in real terms for January 1991 was 0.8% lower than the previous year. Housing construction orders for the same period declined 7.9%, while commercial construction made a gain on the same scale. Public-sector construction also contracted 7%. But this first negative month's result need not be cause for concern, especially as order backlogs climbed from 2.9 months in January 1991 to 3.1 months in February. The largest backlog in the period 1970 to 1989 came in 1970, when construction companies took 3.6 months to process orders.

Development of Construction Volume

Year	Building volume in DM billion	Nominal change from previous year in %	Real change from previous year in %
1990	324.3	11.9	5.4
1989	287.5	8.2	5.0
1988	265.6	6.3	4.7
1987	249.8	2.0	0
1986	244.8	4.5	2.7

Source: German Construction Industry Association

Lower growth can be expected in 1991 for housing construction. This area will nonetheless continue to be the main influence on the industry's growth despite rising prices and high interest rates. Commercial construction remained relatively stable, with 1990 orders up 8.8% on the previous year. Furthermore, the order backlog in January 1991 was still at the record level of 3.8 months, thereby ensuring expansion at the beginning of the year. The lowest increase for 1990 was in public-sector construction, a trend which will continue in 1991.

For the period from 1989 to 1992, German construction companies expect annual growth in real building volume in western Germany to average about 2%. This means that employment in the industry will increase by 1993. According to the Ifo economic research institute, 20% of the companies surveyed still report production problems owing to the shortage of manpower.

Western German construction companies have so far been hesitant about commencing operations in eastern Germany. Ifo discovered that only 3% of all companies did business in eastern Germany in 1990, and this accounted for only 1% of their total output. These low figures are largely the result of caution by western investors, which in turn arises from the numerous – mainly bureaucratic – obstacles to investment. Ifo nonetheless reports that in 1991 around 13% of companies are planning to start activities in eastern Germany, rising to 16% in 1992. It is mainly the larger companies which are expanding their operations in eastern Germany, with business concentrated on overhauling and building up infrastructure in transportation, environmental protection and telecommunications. A further indication of the unsatisfactory state of the eastern German housing construction business is the data made available recently by the Federal Statistical Office. These preliminary figures show that a total of 60,055 new dwellings were built in 1990 in eastern Germany (including eastern Berlin). This is 23,306 or 28% fewer than in 1989. Eastern Berlin scores worst in this shortfall of new housing: 60% fewer dwellings were constructed there in 1990 than in 1989. It can only be hoped for eastern German and western German companies alike that conditions will improve and investment will be encouraged.

Electrical Engineering and Electronics

Strong growth in the electrical engineering and electronics industry in recent years persisted in 1990. Almost all areas benefited from these positive trends, according to ZVEI, the industry's national body, so that the gap between capital goods and consumer durables diminished. Capital goods, the industry's most important segment, recorded 6% growth in 1990. At 7%, growth in consumer durables was again above average.

The industry's fortunes generally reflect the situation in mechanical engineering and vehicle manufacturing: while the domestic climate was favourable, foreign business slackened off. Domestic sales were a nominal 10% higher than in the previous year, while shipments to foreign customers rose only 4%. ZVEI figures indicate that this trend has been apparent since mid-1989. Pent-up demand in eastern Germany mainly affected growth in consumer electronics, and leisure electronics in particular. In this area production shot up 11%.

Weak foreign demand hampered the development of exports. Sales abroad posted a nominal increase of only 1.1%, which translates into stagnation in real terms. The downturn in business was most pronounced with the UK, Denmark and the US, while deliveries to Italy, Spain and Portugal rose at an above-average rate. Exports to Japan also made appreciable gains (15.7%). This had little influence on the overall export figures, however, as the industry's share in aggregate exports to Japan comes to only 2%.

Electrical Engineering and Electronics: 1990 in Figures

1. Sales	
– in DM billion	194.70
– % nominal change 89/90	8.2%
– % real change 89/90	6.9%
2. Exports	
– in DM billion	86.63
– % nominal change 89/90	1.1%
– % real change 89/90	0
3. Imports	
– in DM billion	76.45
– % nominal change 89/90	9.7%
– % real change 89/90	12.5%
4. Workforce	
– in 1,000	1.08
– % change 89/90	2.2%
5. Incoming orders	
– % change 89/90 total	8.5%
– % change 89/90 dom.	9.2%
– % change 89/90 foreign	7.1%

Source: ZVEI

Growth in exports outpaced imports (up 9.7% year-on-year), which kept the import-income ratio down to around 54%, while the export-income ratio fell to 57%. Nonetheless, the export volume of a good DM 86 billion makes this sector one of the enduring pillars of German export business.

The EC electrical engineering and electronics sector, however, is several steps behind the competition in the US and Japan. Despite its high sales, this sector has played a secondary role on the international stage over the last few years. The EC Commission has now published an analysis of the industry in an attempt to arrive at an industry-wide strategy. The Commission blames the industry's weaknesses on its relatively narrow sales markets. Norms and systems intended for domestic markets prove to be an obstacle at the European and international level.

The resulting smaller series saddle EC companies with higher costs than their Japanese and American competitors. Thinking small also means that R&D funding is insufficient and innovation falls short of what is needed. The Commission also sees a further problem in the shortage of highly skilled labour.

ZVEI figures indicate real production growth of 3% to 4% for 1991 in Germany. An upward trend in eastern Germany will be slow to start, though the electrical engineering and electronics industry is one of the sectors to have declined least in recent months. According to ZVEI, the main problems facing eastern German companies are the loss of traditional markets and the lack of marketable products.

Energy

As in many other countries, the energy sector in the Federal Republic of Germany is heavily influenced by government energy policy. The main target is to safeguard energy supplies. The most important domestic source of energy in Germany is hard coal, and its mining continues to be heavily subsidized. In 1990, 71 million tonnes of coal equivalent in hard coal were extracted. An industry optimization model envisages capacity being reduced to 58.7 million tonnes of coal equivalent by 2005. All mines would then be operating optimally.

According to estimates by Arbeitsgemeinschaft Energiebilanzen, (Statistical Commission on Energy), primary energy consumption in western Germany for 1990 rose 1.6% year-on-year to 388.9 million tonnes of coal-equivalent units. By contrast, economic dislocation caused energy consumption in eastern Germany to plunge 18% to 105 million tonnes of coal-equivalent units.

In western Germany the most important fuel was oil, which covered 40.9% of all energy requirements. Hard coal, the second main source, accounted for just short of 19%. In eastern Germany, brown coal dominates with a 68% share. According to the German Coal Mining Association, Germany was dependent on imports for a good half of its energy supplies in 1990. The key imported fuel is oil, 97% of which is supplied from abroad. The second main imported fuel is natural gas, with around three-quarters of all supplies coming from abroad. The importance of foreign suppliers varies according to the use for which the fuel is intended.

Domestic fuel supplies (hard coal, brown coal, hydroelectric power and nuclear power) cover almost 90% of Germany's electricity requirements. But this is less a reflection of sound economic reasoning than of government energy policy and the related purchase commitments. In 1980, 44 electricity companies and the mine operators signed the *Jahrhundertvertrag* calling for the electricity companies to raise their purchases of domestically produced hard coal by 1 million tonnes a

Primary Energy Consumption in 1990

Western Germany	Eastern Germany	United Germany
389 million t	105 million t	494 million t
40.9% oil	68.6% brown coal	35.8% oil
18.9% coal	17.1% oil	21.1% brown coal
17.5% natural gas	8.6% natural gas	15.6% natural gas
12.2% nuclear power	3.1% coal	15.5% coal
8.2% brown coal	2.1% nuclear power	10% nuclear power
2.3% hydroelectric power	0.5% hydroelectric power	2% hydroelectric power

Source: Arbeitsgemeinschaft Energiebilanzen

year to 47.5 million tonnes. This undertaking was fixed until 1990; since then coal purchases have been linked to electricity consumption.

Ownership in the electricity industry is characterized by high concentration and a large proportion of regional authorities. Consequently, semi-public enterprises dominate in this area.

Heating, the leading consumer of energy, is almost entirely dependent on imported fuel, principally heating oil and natural gas. Because of its consumption of mineral oil, the transport sector is also heavily dependent on imports. This dependence for heating on imports thrusts particular importance on the origin of fuel imports: 30% of oil imports come from the North Sea, 50% from the OPEC countries and around 8% from the Soviet Union. Experts calculate that OPEC deliveries will increase again in the Nineties. In the case of hard coal, 47% of imports come from South Africa and 24% from Poland.

Unlike western Germany, most fuel in eastern Germany is produced domestically – especially brown coal, which accounts for 80% of all electricity and 58% of all heating. Natural gas and oil are largely imported, mainly from the former Comecon countries.

Energy producers have already recognized the importance of environmental production. It will take on even greater importance in eastern Germany, and presents a real challenge for power engineering.

Mechanical Engineering

For the third year running, plant and machinery manufacturers recorded appreciable growth rates. In terms of sales and exports, no other German industry recorded greater volume in 1990. In the near future, companies are going to be faced with some difficulties, though nothing to challenge the leading role of the sector at home and abroad.

Real 6.1% growth in production in 1990 was chiefly carried by good domestic business, according to VDMA, the industry association. While domestic orders made a year-on-year gain of 6% in real terms, foreign demand slid 7%. Consequently, foreign sales by this traditionally export-oriented sector only climbed a real 0.4% in 1990.

In domestic business, companies profited from the surge in demand from eastern Germany. The recession in many western industrial nations was to blame for the weak development of exports. North America, the UK and Scandinavia moved to the top of the league of countries importing German plant and machinery. Another stumbling block was the virtual absence of demand from Eastern European countries other than eastern Germany and the rise of the D-Mark against the dollar and the yen. This exchange rate development favoured foreign competitors both on their home markets and on outside markets. Imports rose substantially.

VDMA expects modest real production growth approaching 2% in 1991. This estimate is based on the cushion of orders at many companies, averaging about 7 months, and also on continued favourable domestic demand. Mechanical engineering companies will, however, have to reckon with a stronger

Mechanical Engineering 1990 in Figures

1. Sales
– in DM billion   216.24
– % nominal change 89/90   9%
– % real change 89/90   5.3%

2. Exports
– in DM billion   118.76
– % nominal change 89/90 3.5%
– % real change 89/90   0.4%

3. Imports
– in DM billion   60.12
– % nominal
   change 89/90   13.4%
– % real change 89/90   15.3%

4. Workforce
– in 1,000   1,159
– % change 89/90   4.7%

5. Incoming orders
– % change 89/90 total   1%
– % change 89/90 domestic   9%
– % change 89/90 foreign   -5%

Source: VDA

decline than in the past of their domestic business as a result of lower sales and capital spending in other sectors.

The overall slide in business for the plant and machinery sector during 1991 will, however, also have its bright side: for years companies had to struggle with delivery deadlines because of insufficient capacity to meet demand. Thus, part of the market had to be abandoned to competitors. The less promising outlook for growth in 1991 will ease this problem. Capacity utilization was already down from 93% in March 1990 to 90% in December, according to VDMA figures.

The downturn in new orders from abroad means exports are likely to sink 3-4% in real terms during 1991. Foreign business for mechanical engineering companies could receive a boost from the brighter capital investment climate since the Gulf War ended and the D-Mark lost ground to the dollar. On the down side, the mechanical engineering industry is being hampered by tighter export controls introduced after certain German manufacturers were discovered to have made semi-legal technology exports to Iraq. In general, VDMA says that plant and machinery manufacturers are in favour of export controls for sensitive goods to problem countries, but uniform international regulations are needed in order to prevent competition being distorted.

Pharmaceuticals

The pharmaceuticals industry has responded well to recent health reform legislation, especially the flat-fee system for certain products. Sales growth, a decades-old tradition interrupted only in 1986, continued in 1990. Preliminary figures show a good 5% increase in net output. On the other hand, prices for pharmaceuticals prescribed at the cost of the statutory health insurance funds fell 0.1%. This is mainly due to the 11.6% price decrease for drugs subject to flat fees. Prices of drugs which do not yet come under the flat-fee rules climbed 2.7% in 1990.

Export business is an important pillar of the pharmaceuticals industry. German companies exported drugs worth DM 8.85 billion from January to October 1990, a 4.3% increase on the first ten months of 1989. But the value of imports was also up a substantial 8.7% in that period, totalling DM 5.05 billion. In other words, imports grew twice as fast as exports.

There is nothing to prevent further growth of the western German pharmaceuticals market. Companies will try to recoup earnings with new drugs, now that the flat-fee system has reduced income from preparations already on the market. In international competition, research pressures show no signs of letting up. Industry analysts foresee a bright future for any company that achieves a breakthrough in the treatment of chronic illnesses such as Alzheimer's disease or AIDS.

The outlook for eastern German drug makers and their 16,000 employees is gloomy: western German drugs are licensed for sale in eastern Germany, but this is not true the other way around. Production plant is hopelessly antiquated and fails to meet the high standards prevailing in western Germany. A thorough overhaul of these companies would require enormous capital investment.

In the GDR, sales of drugs came to roughly DM 3.5 billion, according to industry figures. For 1991, health insurance funds are expected to have to pay up to DM 5 billion for drugs. Local manufacturers still command about 80% of the eastern German market, as doctors largely prescribe drugs they are familiar with. But in five to seven years at the latest, prescription practices are likely to come into line with the western German pattern.

Expenditure by Statutory Health Insurance Funds

(January to September 1990)

Expenditure in DM billion	
Hospital care:	33.37
Administration costs:	5.14
Doctors:	18.14
Dentists:	6.09
Dentures:	3.47
Pharmaceuticals:	16.06
Health aids:	6.08

Source: Federal Ministry of Labour

As from 1 January 1990, a price reduction of 55% took effect in the east. It applies to all drugs previously sold in eastern German pharmacies, including eastern German products. Drug makers in eastern Germany sought to offset the reduction by introducing price increases in advance. Western German companies were no longer willing to ship drugs eastward at the new conditions. After negotiations with the Ministry of Labour, however, deliveries were resumed. It was agreed in Bonn that the price reduction would be replaced as early as 1 April by another regulation: the pharmaceuticals industry, wholesalers and pharmacies will cover any deficit in the eastern German health insurance system owing to drug prescriptions. This regulation only applies up to a fixed amount, equivalent to a 25% price reduction. If the shortfall exceeds the agreed amount, drug makers, wholesalers and pharmacies will take over half of the remaining deficit, and health insurance funds the other half.

Andrea Beyer

The German Banking System

I. Philosophy

German banking presents a prime example of the prevailing continental European system of universal, or full-service, banking. In its philosophy, this system contrasts sharply with the compartmentalized banking structure which prevails in the US, the UK and Japan.

In those countries, laws and regulatory policy make a sharp distinction between investment and commercial banking. The regulatory barrier between investment bankers and brokers on the one side and lending institutions on the other is seen as a safeguard against certain inherent conflicts of interest which might otherwise arise when these functions are mixed.

Under the universal banking system, one institution is permitted to engage in nearly all conceivable financial activities: lending, deposit taking, payments transactions, leasing, bond issuing, securities trading, etc. In Germany, the law even defines securities brokerage as a banking business, with the result that universal banks also maintain a monopoly on the function of buying and selling for investors on the German securities exchanges. Naturally, these universal banks may also trade securities, currencies and commodities for their own accounts.

Another important peculiarity of the German system is the absence of any restriction against banks owning other types of businesses. A web of interlocking interests between banks and companies insures that industrial or trading firms with big payrolls will seldom be allowed to fail when their businesses slump. This, incidentally, helps to foster a psychology which is indifferent to broad-based equity ownership because this is not crucial to the financial system.

This banking involvement in industry vastly enhances the prestige and influence of the universal banks, whose directors frequently serve on the supervisory boards of the largest and most powerful companies. Several times during the Eighties, legislative proposals were debated to limit the influence of the universal banks by capping the permissible size of their shareholdings in non-banks as some other major countries have always done.

No such legislation has been adopted. Indeed, the advantages of the universal banking system have become so pronounced in recent years that the regulatory regimes in the US and Japan appear to be moving gradually in this direction.

Despite universal banking, there has always been a de facto separation in Germany between banking and insurance. In the Eighties, however, the rapid evolution and integration of global financial markets fostered an irresistible trend toward one-stop financial supermarkets. This was the demise of the traditional gentlemen's agreement, a sort of non-aggression pact, between German bankers and insurers.

Rapid changes are now in progress in the sphere the Germans call *Allfinanz*. The market-leading German commercial bank launched its own life insurance company. The market-leading insurance group cooperates closely with this bank's closest banking rival in the marketing of insurance products. Other banks and insurers have formed marketing alliances, and one insurance group even purchased one of the larger banks.

One obvious advantage the universal banking system offers in comparison with the bifurcated regimes of the US, Japan and the UK is the stability which comes from diversification. The spectacle of banks or thrifts going belly up in Germany is extremely rare.

When share prices collapse in New York, London or Tokyo, the local and national economies can go into shock. Brokerages close or lay off thousands. When Frankfurt stocks plunge, it is business as usual in Germany, even in the investment banking community, which has many other legs to stand on. Conversely, even German thrifts are better equipped to ride out difficult periods for their dominant credit business because they are also universal banks which generate income from other types of financial services.

Although credit remains the mainstay of universal banks, the importance of fee business has risen sharply in the past decade so that it currently accounts for around 30% of the earnings of some of the biggest full-service banks.

A handful of these universal banks have a virtual monopoly on the very lucrative business of bringing new domestic share issues to market. They own large portfolios of holdings in non-banks and are active in the field of venture capital. They serve as book runners for international bond issues and play a vital role in the domestic placement of government debt. Big universal banks also perform securities and market analyses, portfolio management and investment counselling in addition to their very lively business in trading securities on their own account.

II. Financial Regulation, Policy and the Central Bank

The German central bank, the Frankfurt-based Deutsche Bundesbank, enjoys the much same autonomy as does its US counterpart, the Federal Reserve. Its independence from political authorities is enshrined in the German constitution, although the central bank also has an obligation to support the government's general economic policy. The institution's main mission is to issue currency and to ensure the stability of the currency, the D-Mark. But it has other functions, including banking regulation.

The Bundesbank president is nominated by the chancellor and appointed to his post for a term of eight years. Karl Otto Pöhl, the sitting president, is currently serving his second term; he has decided to retire from the post on 1 October 1991, at which time Helmut Schlesinger will take over. The Bundesbank president also presides over the Zentralbankrat, or Central Bank Council, which exercises a policy-making function in credit and monetary policy similar to that of the Fed's Open Markets Committee.

The Central Bank Council includes the Bundesbank board of directors and the presidents of the state central banks, which are actually branches of the Bundesbank in each state. The absorption of five new states from what had been East Germany into the German federation on unification in 1990 posed a constitutional problem for the Council, which was still being debated in mid-1991. This was because the new states are legally entitled to representation in the Council which currently consists of only 18 members: the seven-member Bundesbank directorate and the presidents of the state central banks of the 11 original states, including Berlin.

While Pöhl and the rest of his directorate have suggested capping the Council's future membership at 14, including all seven Bundesbank directors, no state wishes to sacrifice the seat of its central banker. The new Bundesbank law, which must pass both the Bundestag and the state-dominated Bundesrat, might therefore expand the Council to 22 members, including a seat for each state central bank president. Such a change could hold subtle implications for future credit and monetary policy by diluting the influence of the directorate.

The Central Bank Council sets targets for money supply growth and can influence credit markets by adjusting its discount and Lombard lending rates to banks. The Bundesbank alone conducts open market operations. It requires banks to maintain with it no-yield, minimum reserve deposits. The Bundesbank uses both interest-rate and liquidity-policy instruments, such as weekly securities repurchase agreements, to influence conditions in the money and credit markets as well as the reserve position of the banking system.

The instruments which transmit monetary policy decisions through the universal commercial banking system are highly effective because German banks rely so heavily on the interbank money market for their short-term money management. Thus the Council, which convenes fortnightly, establishes a medium-term rate corridor with its discount and Lombard policy within which the Bundesbank directly tunes the money market's interest and liquidity levels with weekly repurchases, short-term reversible assistance measures and special liquidity interventions.

Watchdog agencies at federal level enforce the federal banking and insurance laws. The banking system is policed in this way by the Bundesbank together with the Bundesaufsichtsamt für das Kreditwesen. The Bundesaufsichtsamt für das Versicherungswesen performs a similar oversight function for insurance companies. The Banking Act prescribes banking supervision, auditing, business activities and liquidity and capital adequacy guidelines for banks.

It was the Bundesbank and the Bundesaufsichtsamt which jointly organized the late 1983 rescue of Schröder, Münchmeyer, Hengst & Co., when this private Hamburg bank became hopelessly overextended because of its lending exposure to a single industrial customer through its offshore credit subsidiary in Luxembourg. It was this spectacular banking collapse which prompted the Bundesbank and Bundesaufsichtsamt to recommend a revision to the banking law. The revised law extended German supervision and lending limits to all the consolidated foreign subsidiaries of German banks by requiring global balance sheets.

It was the Bundesbank which organized and executed the mid-1990 German currency union in which the defunct soft currency of East Germany was replaced by the infusion of around DM 130 billion in hard D-Marks into that region. This unprecedented operation expanded the D-Mark money stock by an amount estimated at between 10% and 15% of the entire West German broad money aggregate.

Led by the Bundesbank, sweeping measures were taken in the Eighties to liberalize the German capital market and to open it to foreign financial intermediaries. During this period of reform, foreign-owned banks were permitted to act as lead managers of D-Mark-denominated Eurobond issues and to participate in the government bond placement consortium.

Foreign banks or brokerages may license German banking subsidiaries which enjoy essentially the same privileges as domestic banks. Prohibitions were dropped on the flotation of floating rate notes and bonds linked to interest or currency swaps. Most recently, the government abolished its onerous turnover tax on securities to make Frankfurt a more attractive base for investment banking.

In May 1990, the Central Bank Council permitted domestic banks to issue bonds denominated in ECUs. It also authorized the private use of Special Drawing Rights (SDR) as it had previously done with ECU. The council further authorized domestic banks to issue foreign currency bonds, an activity that had been restricted to foreign banks in Germany.

Germany, however, has delayed compliance with the EC directive on cross-border marketing of mutual funds to the extent that it continued to bar domestic money market investment funds because these might diminish the effectiveness of the Bundesbank's market-steering policy instruments.

Perhaps the biggest challenge currently facing the banking system is the reorganization and integration of the vastly different banking landscape which prevailed in East Germany until currency union and unification. Another important hurdle is adaptation to proposed unified international and European Community guidelines and regulations on banking and financial markets, including new ratios governing capital adequacy, the definitions of core and soft capital and the definition of a bank itself.

III. Structure of the Banking System

There are currently more than 4,000 banks doing business in western Germany alone, down from more than 13,000 in 1957. But these banks now operate nearly 40,000 domestic branch offices, compared with fewer than 13,000 some 33 years ago. The numbers reflect the large-scale consolidation and reorganization which has occurred in German banking during the postwar period. With one bank branch office for about ever 1,500 citizens, western Germany is regarded as somewhat overbanked and therefore an infertile terrain for new competitors in the retail banking field. Until recently, however, the essential structure of banking has changed little in western Germany.

The German banking system includes public, private and cooperative credit institutions. The three major divisions are the private commercial banks, the savings bank system and the cooperative banking system. There are also building societies, mortgage banks and specialized institutions, which do not operate as universal banks. Even the postal service operates a large retail banking operation at its post offices, which competes with other sectors in deposit taking. Its 1990 assets came to DM 70 billion. The Bundesbank estimated the business volume of all 4,040 banks in western Germany at DM 4.67 trillion the end of 1990.

On the eve of German unification in 1990, some 320 foreign banks from 50 countries were represented in western Germany alone through 60 branches, 90 subsidiaries and around 330 liaison offices. US banks maintained the strongest presence, followed by Japanese and French banks. There were also 21 non-German banks represented in eastern Germany at this time. In western Germany, the foreign-owned banks shared less than 5% of the German market by business volume.

1. Private Commercial Banks. Germany's private commercial banks are full-service universal banks, which are usually organized as joint stock corporations, limited liability companies or general partnerships with shares. At least six of these play a significant international role. The first three have been dubbed the "big three" because of their size and prestige, but two formerly regional branch banks have grown to the point that one could speak of a "big five" in private commercial branch banking.

At the end of 1990, there were 335 active private commercial banks with nearly 7,000 offices, around 200,000 employees and combined assets of close to DM 1.17 trillion. In addition to the "big three" of Deutsche Bank AG, Dresdner Bank AG and Commerzbank AG and their Berlin subsidiaries, this sector encompassed 185 regional and other similar banks, 83 private bankers and 60 branches of foreign banks. Bayerische Vereinsbank AG and Bayerische Hypotheken- und Wechsel-Bank AG (Hypo Bank) are in close pursuit of the volume leaders, making them eligible for inclusion in a new "big five" grouping.

Five leading private commercial banks

	Global assets end of 1990
Deutsche Bank AG	DM 400.2 billion
Dresdner Bank AG	DM 283.3 billion
Commerzbank AG	DM 216.0 billion
Bayerische Vereinsbank AG	DM 205.9 billion
Bayerische Hypotheken- und Wechsel-Bank AG	DM 174.6 billion

All of these big banks have rushed to establish a strong presence in the new eastern states. Deutsche Bank and Dresdner Bank have done so by buying into the extensive branch network of Deutsche Kreditbank (DKB), which in a March 1990 reform was assigned control of the commercial operations of East Germany's former Staatsbank, or state bank. Deutsche invested DM 1 billion to obtain 122 DKB branches and 8,500 staff. Dresdner paid DM 500 million into its joint venture with DKB and set up another 35 branches on its own.

Commerzbank opted to set up its own 50-branch eastern German network from the ground up with a projected investment of around DM 150 million. Even before political unification it said its eastern German operation had 80,000 customers, assets of DM 6 billion and DM 2 billion in deposits. Berliner Handels- und Frankfurter Bank (BHF), meanwhile, took a controlling interest in eastern Germany's Deutsche Handelsbank (DHB).

Private commercial banking is also the sector of German banking which maintains the highest international profile. Deutsche Bank has ranked as high as 10th or 15th on international banking lists in recent years. Dresdner Bank is about 10 places behind and Commerzbank 15 places further back among the global "top 100" in assets.

Of the 407 foreign operations run by all German banks at the start of 1991, 185 are maintained by the "big three" and another 102 were set up by the regional banks and 19 by private banks. Only 96 of the 407 foreign subsidiaries, branches or offices of German banks were organized by banks in sectors other than private commercial banking. Germany's foreign banking outposts are concentrated overwhelmingly in Europe and America. Luxembourg, with nearly three dozen German offshore banks, is a leading Euro-DM centre.

Large and prominent private commercial banks which are somewhat smaller than the "big five" include Bank für Gemeinwirtschaft AG, Berliner Handels- und Frankfurter Bank KGaA, Berliner Bank AG and Westfalenbank AG. Vereins- und Westbank AG, which would have been next on the list, merged into Bayerische Vereinsbank in mid-1990.

The entire sector of private commercial banking has a share of about 25% in the overall assets of all German banks. The share for the "big three" alone is around 9%. Commerzbank, the smallest of the top three, has a share of about 2% in the German lending business.

Large German subsidiaries of foreign banks are also prominent players in this sector. A few of them are KKB Bank AG (Citibank), Trinkhaus & Burkhardt KGaA (Midland), Schweizerische Kreditanstalt (Deutschland) AG, J P Morgan GmbH, Schweizerischer Bankverein (Deutschland) AG, Merck, Finck und Co. KG (Barclays) and Bank Julius Bär (Deutschland) AG. Among foreign banks with the largest German branches were Fuji Bank Ltd., Morgan Guaranty Trust Co., Banco di Napoli, Bank of Tokyo Ltd. and Sanwa Bank Ltd.

The foreign commercial banks were quick to move into the new eastern German market. Citicorp set up liaison offices in eastern Berlin, Dresden and

Leipzig. Salomon Brothers and Barclays opened offices in eastern Berlin and Bank of Tokyo won permission to establish a branch there.

2. Savings Bank (Sparkassen) System. This important German banking sector has been essentially a two-tiered system which included at the end of 1990 in western Germany alone 575 savings banks (Sparkassen), each a universal bank, and ten regional central institutions (Landesbanken), plus Deutsche Girozentrale - Deutsche Kommunalbank (DGZ). DGZ performs some central bank clearing functions for the sector, although it would overstate the case somewhat to classify it as the central bank for the whole system.

The regional central banks also usually serve as house banks for their respective state governments. The Sparkassen, ranging from tiny banks to some giant metropolitan branch banks with international connections, held assets of DM 979 billion at the end of 1990. These banks maintain around 17,000 branch offices throughout western Germany. There they account for nearly 23% of all lending to businesses and private persons and 32% of all non-bank deposits.

Their regional central institutions together with DGZ balanced assets of DM 762 billion. DGZ in 1990 was in the process of setting up a fully owned subsidiary called Ostdeutsche Landesbank to serve as the regional central institution for 196 East German Sparkassen savings banks which entered the system on unification.

Ostdeutsche Landesbank was estimated to have assets of DM 145 billion following currency union. This DGZ transitional arrangement was jeopardized in 1991 when the eastern state of Thüringen decided to pool its thrift organization with its prosperous western neighbour, the state of Hessen, instead. This seemed to open the gates for a series of east-west partnerships among the regional thrift organizations.

The recent history of the thrifts sector in western Germany has also been marked by dissent, including infighting in the ranks and among the three echelons of its hierarchy. Some of the largest and most influential urban savings banks have set up their own supra-regional and international organizations, bypassing their regional central banks. And a whole raft of proposed mergers among the system's regional central banks have collapsed because of political rivalries. Among the larger western German branch savings banks were the independent Hamburger Sparkasse, the Sparkasse der Stadt Berlin-West, Landesgirokasse Stuttgart, Stadtsparkasse Köln and Nassauische Sparkasse Wiesbaden. Frankfurter Sparkasse, a recent merger product of one thrift within the system and another which was independent, is one of the biggest independent savings banks in Germany.

Among the central institutions of the savings bank system, Westdeutsche Landesbank Girozentrale (WestLB) is easily the largest with assets approaching

DM 200 billion. Although WestLB is strictly a wholesale bank without a retail operation inside western Germany, it has a formidable international network. WestLB in the late Eighties bought the foreign branch network of Britain's Standard Chartered Bank. As unification approached, it took a controlling interest in an eastern German joint venture with Deutsche Aussenhandelsbank, formerly part of East Germany's all-powerful Staatsbank. The venture, called Deutsche Industrie- und Handelsbank, had 200 branches and 1,200 employees at the end of 1990.

Other large central banks in the thrift sector include Bayerische Landesbank Girozentrale, Norddeutsche Landesbank Girozentrale, Hessische Landesbank Girozentrale and Südwestdeutsche Landesbank Girozentrale.

3. Cooperative System of Raiffeisenbanken and Volksbanken. DG-Deutsche Genossenschaftsbank (DG Bank), with global assets of around DM 193 billion at the end of 1990, is the central bank of a German credit cooperative system which has included regional central banks and thousands of local western German credit cooperatives, each a universal bank. The system is in the process of being reorganized into two tiers with the absorption of the regional central institutions by DG Bank, which plays an international role and usually ranks among the top 50 on world lists of banking assets. DG Bank has also stepped into the role of central bank for the eastern German cooperative credit system. The 95 urban and 272 rural credit co-ops in the new eastern states were invited to buy shares in the central bank just as the western co-ops also participate in the system.

The 3,049 individual western German credit cooperatives, which cater especially to the banking needs of tradesmen and farmers, had combined assets of DM 563 billion at the end of 1990. There are few rural market centres without a Raiffeisenbank, which caters to farmers, or cities and towns without a Volksbank, which serves the needs of tradesmen or professionals in particular.

In western Germany, the local credit cooperatives handle more than 12% of all lending to non-banking businesses and private citizens and receive nearly 20% of their deposits. A few large members of the cooperative credit system are Deutsche Apotheker- und Ärztebank eG, Badische Beamtenbank eG, Berliner Volksbank (West) eG, Stuttgarter Bank AG and Südwestbank AG.

Edward Roby

Incentives to Invest in Eastern Germany

The federal government is encouraging commercial investments in the new *Länder* through depreciation allowances, various types of investment grants and tax incentives. Considerable emphasis is being put on stimulating the *Mittelstand* (small and medium-sized companies) with favourable loans for business startups, modernization of existing facilities and environmental protection measures.

Public authorities are trying to expedite project approval, and eastern Germany is growing more investor-friendly. Three developments suggest that the major barriers to investing in the new *Länder* have been breached. Firstly, there are now clearer guidelines regarding ownership of property and property disputes. Investors are often given priority when their claim conflicts with that of private individuals. Secondly, the Treuhandanstalt (the public trust authority which regulates privatizations; see pages 115-120) has speeded up its activities; the faster it privatizes, the faster it pulls in funds which it can use to write-off eastern German company debts – the second most serious investment deterrent after property disputes. Thirdly, the Soviet pledge to import DM 9 billion worth of goods from eastern Germany will secure sufficient cash flow for many companies in the medium term. This vastly reduces the financial burden of western buyers or participants in a joint venture. The industries most likely to benefit are those exporting rolling stock, ships, agricultural machinery, mining equipment, foodstuffs and certain light industrial products.

Investments in infrastructure will be supported by billions of D-Mark over the next few years, and through a programme called *Gemeinschaftswerk Aufschwung Ost* the federal government has allocated an additional DM 24 billion up to the end of 1992 to further investments and the creation of jobs in the new *Länder*. Investments of DM 1 million in new offices or equipment in the east can elicit DM 230,000 in government aid. Half of the investment can be written off from the taxable profit as extraordinary depreciation. The profitability of an investment can be increased by almost half, and up to 40% of the promoting measures will be realized within the first year of the expenditures.

Investment Subsidies

Public investment subsidies for ventures in eastern Germany can be divided into two categories: those to which the investor is legally entitled (investment grants); and those which are allocated on a discretionary basis.

Direct Grants (Investitionszulagen). Direct investment grants are paid in cash and any applicant who fulfils the prerequisites is legally entitled to such a grant, which is generally awarded regardless of turnover, success, type of industry or location. All taxpayers (resident or non-resident) are entitled to apply.

Not all investments qualify. Investments must be for the acquisition and/or manufacture of depreciable and moveable goods (machinery or office equipment). The purchase cost may not be lower than DM 800 and the goods must be booked on the company balance sheet. Intangible goods such as patents or licences do not qualify for these types of grants, nor does the purchase of passenger cars. The goods must remain a fixed part of the factory or plant in the new *Länder* for at least three years following their acquisition or manufacture. The size of the grant varies:

- Grants for investments made between 1 July 1990 and 31 December 1991 amount to 12% of purchase or production cost.
- Grants for investments made between 1 January 1992 and 31 December 1994 amount to 8%.
- Goods that have been delivered or produced after 31 December 1992 can only qualify for the grants if the applicants ordered them or began to produce them prior to 1 January 1993.

An investment counts as completed once the goods have been delivered or the production cost incurred. The subsidies are all tax-free.

Separate applications must be made for different capital goods, thus making multiple applications commonplace. Investment grants do not preclude other federal subsidies. Applications must be submitted after the initiation of the investment, but no later than 30 September of the following fiscal year. The local *Finanzämter* (tax offices) provide the necessary forms and process the applications. The federal government estimates that these benefits will result in a loss of potential tax revenue totalling DM 400 million in 1991 and DM 650 million in 1992. For further general information, contact the Finance Ministry:

Bundesministerium der Finanzen, Graurheindorfer Str. 108, W-5300 Bonn 1, Tel: (0228) 6 82-0; Fax: (0228) 6 82-44 20; -44 66

Investment Allowances (Investitionszuschüsse). The five new *Länder* have become part of a federal programme which grants aid for regional development. For five years, the new *Länder* have been given special status whereby they can receive up to DM 3 billion annually to provide a framework for private investment. The regional subsidies are allocated on a discretionary basis due to the limited resources made available by the federal government. Those who qualify for assistance are most easily defined by the sectors which are excluded: agriculture and fishing, energy and water supply, mining, construction, retailing (except mail order), consumer goods wholesaling, transport and warehousing, hospitals and convalescence centres. There is a long list of "positive designations" which can be ordered from Verlag Dr. Hans Heger, Postfach 201363, W-5300 Bonn 2 (ask for Bundesdrucksache Nr. 11/7501; 19. Rahmenplan der Gemeinschaftsaufgabe). The subsidies vary according to the nature of the project.

- Investments for the establishment of a business in municipalities where the company does not already operate are eligible for up to 23% of costs.
- The same rate applies to the acquisition of a company which has been closed down, or one threatened with bankruptcy.
- Capacity expansions which increase employment by over 15% or 50 full-time positions can obtain up to 20%.
- Streamlining and restructuring measures receive up to 15%.

Intangible goods are not excluded but are not a high priority. The percentages given above are maximum subsidies allocated according to local guidelines which vary between *Länder* and municipalities. Hence it makes sense to discuss particular requirements with the appropriate official at the local *Finanzamt*, especially since applications for subsidies must be made *before the start of the project*. This places considerable demands on the investor, since he must submit precise estimates of projected costs and staffing levels. Overestimates may be penalized by the curtailment of the subsidies. Investment allowances may be supplemented by 12% with non-regional subsidies.

Applications must be submitted before 1 July 1995. Addresses of the relevant authorities in the *Länder* can be obtained from the Berlin office of the Economics Ministry:

Bundesministerium für Wirtschaft, Außenstelle Berlin, Unter den Linden 44-60, O-1080 Berlin, Tel: (030) 3 99 85-0; Fax: (030) 3 99 85-250.

Special Depreciation Allowances. Special depreciation allowances may be applicable in the case of the purchase and manufacture of depreciable moveable and non-moveable income-producing assets and for building extensions. A further list of what may be eligible for these depreciation allowances is given in the draft of the 1991 tax reform act (Bundestags-Drucksache 12/219). Assets which are accorded special depreciation may not be used privately more than 10% of the time. Due to a change in the law, special depreciation may be claimed in combination with investment grants. All taxpaying companies and private individuals are eligible to apply. The special depreciation amounts to 50% of the purchase or production cost of the assets and can be claimed in the year of purchase/production and in the four years thereafter. Special depreciation already applies to instalment payments on acquisition costs and part of the production costs. Assets must have been purchased or produced (in part or in toto) or buildings (in part or in toto) erected after 31 December 1990 and prior to 1 January 1995. For further information, contact the local *Finanzamt* or the Finance Ministry at the address listed above.

Research and Development Subsidies. The Federal Ministry of Research and Technology (BMFT) has several promotion programmes for companies which contract out R&D work in order to develop new production technologies and/or products for small and medium-sized companies which are already operating in eastern Germany. The R&D is expected to generate economic gain. It must involve "high" technological and financial risks to be worthy of subsidy.

Other programmes aim at bolstering R&D departments in small and medium-sized enterprises in the new *Länder*. Amounts of subsidies are currently being decided. For further information, contact Referat II/6 of the Berlin office of the Economics Ministry (see address above) or the main office in Bonn: Bundesministerium für Wirtschaft, Referat II C 1, Villemombler Str. 76, W-5300 Bonn 1, Tel: (0228) 6 15-1; Fax: (0228) 6 15-44 36; -44 37

The Ministry of Research and Technology has started a pilot project to promote the founding of new high-tech oriented businesses. The programme seeks to further the establishment of technology centres, to stimulate employment in R&D, to promote contracted research and consulting regarding innovations for companies. So far, the subsidies available are unspecified. For more information, contact the main or the Berlin office of the Ministry of Research and Technology: Bundesministerium für Forschung und Technologie, Heinemannstr. 2 W-5300 Bonn-Bad Godesberg, Tel: (0228) 59-0; Fax: (0228) 59-36 01

Bundesministerium für Forschung und Technologie
Außenstelle Berlin, Hannoversche Str. 30, O-1040 Berlin
Tel: (030) 39 98 10-0; Fax: (030) 39 98 10-2 70

Consulting Subsidies. In an effort to accelerate the introduction of western managerial and technical know-how into eastern Germany, the government is willing to pay up to 80% of consultant fees, albeit only DM 3,000 per project, or DM 9,000 to a given company. The funds may be deployed for general management consulting as well as professional advice on environmental issues, energy-savings and business startups. It is the consultant who should apply for the benefits before 31 May of the calendar year following the consultation. Eligibility is limited to consultants whose business is located in western Germany or western Berlin or who have a branch there. For further information and application forms, contact the Federal Office of Economics:
Bundesamt für Wirtschaft, Postfach 5171, W-6236 Eschborn
Tel: (06196) 4 04-0; Fax: (06196) 4 04-2 12

Loans and Guarantees

All special credit facilities for firms active in eastern Germany are available to foreign investors, provided they own all or part of a company registered in the new *Länder*. At first glance, it may appear that certain programmes exclude benefits for large companies with annual turnover exceeding DM 500 million. However, these limits apply only to operations on eastern German territory. Government loan guarantees are available for all sizes of investment.

ERP Programmes. Small and medium-sized companies *(Mittelstand)* and private persons investing in eastern Germany can take advantage of loans from the Federal Republic and paid out of the European Recovery Programme. These long-term, reduced-interest loans focus on investment promotion in the areas of:

- Tourism (to support the construction, extension and modernization of hotels, inns and restaurants).
- Business startups (to encourage the establishment and purchase of enterprises and professional services; the loans cover startup investments in the first three years of operations).
- Environmental protection (for water purification, waste reduction, recycling, the reduction of air pollution, energy-savings and the use of renewable energy sources).

- Modernization (for the improvement of existing plant and machinery – machines, vehicles, buildings – and expansion of production facilities; to increase productivity by enhancing in-company know-how).

ERP loans have the following key features:
- Reduced interest rates which are not subject to change (currently 7.5% per annum).
- Long maturities of up to 15 years for fixed asset investments and 20 years for construction projects.
- Five-year grace period for repayment, after which repayments are due every six months.

Usually the credit ceiling for all investment projects is fixed at DM 300,000. ERP credits are awarded on the proviso that the project would otherwise be "substantially handicapped". ERP credits do not provide one-stop investment financing: for companies with annual turnover of up to DM 10 million the maximum financing amounts to 50% of the sum invested; for companies with higher turnover, the financing amount is usually not more than one-third of the investment. Applicants from eastern Germany are given higher credit ceilings of up to DM 1 million (with 50% maximum financing).

Eligible applicants are domestic enterprises and professionals, foreign enterprises establishing an independent branch in the new *Länder* or investing in an enterprise there, or private individuals who wish to found a company. Annual turnover of the company (group) may not exceed DM 50 million. However, companies with annual turnover of up to DM 500 million are entitled to apply for loans for environmental protection measures on favourable terms.

Applications for loans can be made through any German bank, which acts as a guarantor and checks the application. Once it agrees to the strategic approach, it passes on the application to one of the following three institutions which act on behalf of the ERP programme for the Federal Republic:
Kreditanstalt für Wiederaufbau
Palmengartenstr. 5-9, W-6000 Frankfurt/M 1
Tel: (069) 74 31-0; Fax: (069) 74 31-29 44.

Deutsche Ausgleichsbank
Wielandstr. 4, W-5300 Bonn 2, Tel: (0228) 8 31-1; Fax: (0228) 8 31- 2 55

Berliner Industriebank
Landecker Str. 2, W-1000 Berlin 33, Tel: (030) 82 00 30; Fax: (030) 8 24 30 03

Other Loan Programmes. The *Kreditanstalt für Wiederaufbau,* or KfW (German Reconstruction Loan Corporation) was founded in 1948 as part of the Marshall Plan. It grants loans with long maturities and is one of the ten largest banks in the Federal Republic. It offers three loan programmes to promote economic development in eastern Germany:

- The *Mittelstand* programme is designed for companies with turnover below DM 500 million. Funds must be used to start up a business, expand capacity or streamline operations. Sums of up to DM 10 million or two-thirds of the investment are paid out. Repayment is due over up to 10 years and there is a two-year grace period on repaying the principal. The interest rate is fixed at the time of lending (currently 8%) and 96% of the loan is paid out directly.
- The environmental protection programme supports any type of investment in water purification, recycling and waste disposal, energy-savings and measures to combat noise or air pollution. A company of any size may apply for credits of up to DM 10 million, or two-thirds of the investment. Interest and repayment conditions are the same as for the first programme, except that the currently available fixed rate is 7.5%.
- The residential housing modernization programme is open both to companies and private individuals. Funds can be used to modernize or repair housing which is rented or owned. Loans do not generally exceed DM 500 per sq metre. Repayment can be made over a period of up to 25 years, and the borrower enjoys a five-year grace period before having to start to repay the principal. The interest rate is fixed for the first ten years. For this programme, it is important that applications be filed before the investment is initiated.

In the case of investments with "especially high value" for the economy of the new *Länder,* companies with higher annual turnover than the ones given above may be considered. For further information, contact Mr. Genter of the KfW at the address given above.

Programmes run by the *European Investment Bank* (EIB) carry terms offered on the capital markets. Projects in eastern Germany generally fall within the scope of the EIB's overall commitment to developing economically weak regions in the EC. Credits are typically provided for investments in infrastructure (transport and communications), environmental protection, environmental research and improvements to international competitiveness. Credits up to about 10 million ECUs (about DM 20 million), or 50% of investment costs, can be applied for through the Industriekreditbank (Postfach 1118, W-4000 Düsseldorf 1, tel: (0211) 82 21-0) or the Berliner Industriebank (Postfach 11 05 80, W-1000 Berlin

11, tel: (030) 8 20 03-0). Larger sums enter the league of conventional project finance, and are dealt with by the EIB itself. Maturities range from seven to 12 years for industrial credits and run up to 20 years for infrastructure projects and energy-saving measures. Interest rates are determined by market conditions obtained by the EIB plus 0.15% for expenses.

For more information, contact EIB in Luxembourg:

Europäische Investitionsbank

100, Boulevard Konrad Adenauer, L-2950 Luxembourg

Tel: (32 2) 43 97-1; Fax: (32 2) 43 77 04

Deutsche Ausgleichsbank (Bank for German Settlements) credits are offered under conditions similar to those of the KfW – a 95% initial payout, repayment over ten years at a fixed interest rate (8% at present). Similar projects are eligible. However, the maximum loan is only about DM 1.5 million. Small and medium-sized companies and professionals are entitled to apply. Credits can be combined with subsidies from the equity capital support programme (*Eigenkapitalhilfe*) or ERP loans. Applications can be made via any German bank, which underwrites the facility. For further information, contact the office of the Ausgleichsbank at the address given above, or its Berlin office:

Deutsche Ausgleichsbank, Niederlassung Berlin

Sarrazinstr. 11-15, W-1000 Berlin 41

Tel: (030) 8 50 85-0; Fax: (030) 8 50 85-2 99

Both *banking consortia* and the *federal government* are offering to underwrite credits which fulfil appropriate evaluation standards. Credits of up to DM 1 million for use by the *Mittelstand* are underwritten by banking consortia. Sums of DM 1 million to DM 20 million can receive up to 80% state guarantees, provided that the participating bank is willing to cover at least 20%. Guarantees for credits exceeding DM 20 million are subject to the vague stipulation that the project should serve the general economic interest. Essentially this relates to job creation and/or the promotion of infrastructure, strategic industries and high technology. Applications may be filed through any major German bank. For information on additional federal guarantees, contact:

Treuarbeit AG

Auf'm Hennekamp 47, W-4000 Düsseldorf 1

Tel: (0221) 33 94-1; Fax: (0221) 33 94-2 60

Equity Capital Support Programme. Credits under this programme are designed to buttress the equity base of *Mittelstand* projects considered to have potential. Projects deemed worthy of support include the establishment of a private business or practice, the acquisition of an enterprise or an individual company site, investments geared to strengthen a private company as well as follow-up investments within three years after the initial equity capital support was provided. Anyone under the age of 50 who can show proof of appropriate professional or commercial qualifications may apply under this programme. Applications must be made by 31 December 1993. Credits have a maturity of 20 years (there is a grace period of ten years for the first repayment). No interest has to be paid in the first three years, after which interest rates increase continuously. No collateral is required. Only those projects which will be the main focus of the applicant's professional activities will be considered. Personal equity should be 15% of the basis of valuation. Equity capital support can upgrade this basis to 40% of the basis of valuation. Other financing must be obtained for the additional 60%. The credit ceiling is DM 350,000 (in special cases, DM 400,000). Plans are under way to raise the ceiling to DM 1 million. Applications can be forwarded through any major German bank to the Deutsche Ausgleichsbank. Further information is available from the Economics Ministry.

EC Subsidies

Further subsidies are available from the European Community but have yet to be clearly specified. There is, for example, no hard and fast ruling on simultaneous dual (German and EC) funding. There are, however, programmes which have been laid down in general terms: the EC regional fund (EFRE in German) offers subsidies of up to 50% for investments in business activities and infrastructure. It includes wage payments of up to DM 60,000 per capita/per annum. Both the service and industrial sectors are eligible. The development of tourism has been accorded special attention. EFRE funds will amount to DM 1 billion per annum between 1991 and 1993. Employee training is subsidized at a rate of up to 20% by the European Social Fund (ESF). The coverage includes such activities as advertising and administration, but excludes the cost of buildings. "Trans-national measures" involving exchanges of know-how with other EC countries are specifically promoted.

Laws to Ease Privatization and Stimulate Investment. Critical attention has been focused on amending eastern German property ownership legislation. Many had hoped for an outright reversal of the existing rule regarding conflicting claims on property – which currently gives priority to repossession as opposed to compensation. Instead, politicians voted for exceptions to the existing rule.

Nonetheless, public authorities now have the right to give priority to an investor's claim to property over that of a private claim if the investment furthers economic reconstruction.

Tax Breaks

As of 1 January 1991, West German tax laws were generally applicable to eastern Germany. As a number of tax breaks expire, two important breaks continue to apply. One is that losses attributable to an eastern German shareholding or subsidiary can be offset against taxes paid on profits in western Germany. The key prerequisites are that the stake in the eastern company must be at least 10% and must be acquired between 31 Dec. 1989 and 1 Jan. 1992. While this tax break can be used for up to five years, it cannot exceed the declared value of the equity participation. Secondly, companies operating in western Germany and wishing to sell off plant and equipment can avoid tax on the sale by selling to a company based in eastern Germany. The sale must occur between 31 Dec. 1989 and 1 Jan. 1992, and the tax break must be claimed within ten years thereafter. The Bundestag has recently given its approval to other major decisions on tax breaks. Perhaps the most important decision for investors is the tax exemption in 1991 and 1992 for capital, property, and working capital in the new *Länder*. Taxes on capital and property as well as corporate income tax will resume from 1993 onward.

The following booklets provide further information on the various incentives to invest in the new *Länder:*
*   *Wirtschaftliche Förderung in den neuen Bundesländern.*
    This booklet, published by the Economics Ministry, discusses business promotion in the new *Länder* and reflects the situation as of May 1991. It is due to be issued in English and French and can be obtained free of charge from the ministry's public relations department at Villemombler Str. 76, W-5300 Bonn 1, tel: (0228) 615-1; Fax: (0228) 6 15-44 36; -4437.
*   Not much older is *Doing Business in the Five New German Länder*, published by the Federal Office of Foreign Trade Information. Single orders from abroad are free of charge, otherwise the booklet costs DM 15. It can be obtained from the Federal Office of Foreign Trade (BfAI) at Agrippastr. 87-93, Postfach 10 80 07, W-5000 Cologne 1, tel: (0221) 20 57-0; Fax: (0221) 20 57-2 12; -2 75.

Ilka Eßmüller

The Treuhandanstalt

The Treuhandanstalt is the world's biggest employer. Directly after unification, it gained authority over 9,000 companies, 1.7 million hectares of agricultural land, 1.9 million hectares of forest and 46,000 hectares of formerly state-owned farms. The Treuhandanstalt is the public trust authority charged with reorganizing and selling what had been state-owned East German companies to domestic and foreign investors. The Treuhand can modernize enterprises and give them a more competitive structure, and is empowered to close companies which are not expected to survive on the market.

Not an easy task, and the Treuhand has come under severe criticism. For some, it has privatized too slowly, for others, too fast and without taking into sufficient account the needs of the eastern Germans. After the 1991 assassination of Treuhand president Detlev Karsten Rohwedder, criticism became temporarily muted. By 31 May 1991, the Treuhand had privatized 2,140 companies. The 544 companies privatized in May alone set a new record; by the end of 1990, the Treuhand had sold only 469 formerly state-owned companies, plus numerous restaurants and small retail stores. Of the 544 companies privatized in May, 172 were sold by the Treuhand central office, 372 by its regional offices. The head office generated 85% of the intake of DM 9.5 billion.

Most of the privatized companies are in consumer-oriented sectors such as trade, the automobile industry, foodstuffs and semi-luxury products. Investment pledges amount to DM 61.8 billion and long-term investments in the energy sector alone reach DM 30 billion, according to the Treuhand. The new owners have guaranteed 467,126 jobs. On the negative side: by the end of May 1991, 312 companies had been shut down.

By the end of April 1991, 46 companies had been sold to 50 foreign investors from France, Sweden, the US, the UK and Austria. The Danish sugar company Danisco Dankse Sukkerfabrikken has bought two sugar factories; according to *Handelsblatt*, the business daily, the Danes want to invest DM 319 million in the new assets. Coca Cola has started up operations in Halle.

For one reason or another, foreign investment has fallen far short of expectations. As one means to increase foreign interest in eastern German com-

In May 1991, Hoppenstedt Verlag published a handbook listing 6,000 eastern German firms offered for sale by the Treuhand. This official Treuhand directory contains the most detailed information on eastern German companies yet available from a single source. The price of the 590-page opus is DM 350. The *Offizielles Firmenverzeichnis der Treuhandanstalt* (German title) can be ordered by phone or fax from:

Verlag Hoppenstedt & Co., Postfach 40 06, W-6100 Darmstadt 1

Tel: (06151) 380-1; Fax: (06151) 380-360

panies, the Treuhand is working out new marketing and sales strategies such as the involvement of international investment banks in selling "packages of companies" as reported by the *Süddeutsche Zeitung*. Prominent Treuhand personalities (including president Birgit Breuel) have paid promotional visits to various European countries, the US, Japan and Australia. Jacques Delors, president of the EC Commission, and Breuel agreed at the beginning of June 1991 to supply the European data bank network with information on companies still awaiting a buyer.

Nevertheless, there is a feeling among many would-be foreign investors that their investment is not as welcome as it is being proclaimed to be; that unnecessary hurdles (compounded by the Treuhand) confront them at every turn, and that unless they operate through established western German channels, it is not worth their time, effort and money to move into eastern Germany. The suspicion is voiced that the Germans want to keep their fingers in every eastern German pie.

The Treuhand is under the direct supervision of the Finance Ministry, but acts independently. Many of its staff have been seconded by western German industry, banks and other organizations. The Treuhand also engages its own managers.

The companies that the Treuhand heads can be divided into two categories, those with fewer and those with more than 1,500 employees on the payroll. Only one-third of the 9,000 companies which the Treuhand took over initially employed more than 1,500 people, and these are processed by the head office. The remaining 6,000 companies are handled by the 15 regional offices. Of those companies, 75% have fewer than 250 employees, 20% between 250 and 750, and 6% between 750 and 1,500.

The Treuhand is interested in a complete takeover of a company by the purchaser; it tries not to retain a minority holding. In the case of competing bids, the criteria for making a decision include the proposed corporate strategy, the projected investment volume, the timeframe, the number of jobs that will be created and maintained, the solvency of the prospective buyer and the purchase price. An important means to determine the intrinsic value of the company is the result of the opening balance sheet in D-Marks which eastern companies have to supply.

When the choice is difficult, the Treuhand is "generally willing" to give priority to a management buyout proposal (purchase of a company by its management). MBOs, however, are usually only feasible for smaller companies. MBOs and transformations into stock corporations are viewed by the Treuhand as equally good concepts for privatization.

The Treuhand generally exempts investors from restitution claims and claims for compensation and is also willing to exempt them from all or part of the costs of environmental damages. Federal environmental protection regulations are applicable to eastern Germany; however, the Unification Treaty provides for transitional regulations to modernize already existing plants. The companies under Treuhand authority are as eligible for federal subsidies and investment grants as are private companies.

Foreign investors are advised to seek the aid of a specialist to handle the preliminaries and provide professional assistance in the acquisition process. The purchase normally takes place according to the regulations of the German Civil Code (BGB) and an agreement between the parties.

It may also be advisable to employ German-speaking managers who have worked in western Germany. Skilled labour is available in the eastern *Länder*, especially in technical and handicraft sectors. However, skills in accounting, data processing, new technologies and business management (none of which were needed under the old system) are lacking – a problem due to be remedied by extensive subsidized training schemes already in place.

In addition to other economic data, the following data banks contain information on companies being sold by the Treuhand:

Geneos Wirtschaftsdatenbank
Handelsblatt GmbH
Postfach 11 02, Kasernenstr. 67,
W-4000 Düsseldorf 1
Tel: (0211) 8 87-15 24;
Fax: (0211) 8 87-15 20
(Geneos is the most widely used German system.)

BTX Südwest Datenbank GmbH
Plienninger Str. 150,
W-7000 Stuttgart 80

Tel: (0711) 7 20 07 03;
Fax: (0711) 7 28 92 50

ZVK/CB-Infobank
Postfach 10 05 05,
W-6000 Frankfurt/M 1
Tel: (069) 13 62 36 15;
Fax: (069) 13 62 34 22

DAFNE Data Bank
CD-ROM Verlag & Vertriebs GmbH
Am Hauptbahnhof 12,
W-6000 Frankfurt/M 1
Tel: (069) 27 10 02 58;
Fax: (069) 27 10 02 10
(DAFNE will have information on Treuhand companies starting in 1992.)

Offices of the Treuhandanstalt

The following information on the Treuhand offices has been provided by the Treuhandanstalt and is current as of 6 June 1991:

Treuhandanstalt (main office)
Leipziger Str. 5-7, O-1086 Berlin
Tel: (030) 31 54-01; Fax: (030) 31 54-13 20

Treuhandanstalt (Bonn office)
Bundeskanzlerplatz 2-10, W-5300 Bonn 1
Tel: (0228) 21 10 63; Fax: (0228) 21 52 76

Regional Offices:

Berlin
Schneeglöckchenstr. 26, O-1055 Berlin
Tel: (00 37 2) 4 34 26 01;
car phone: (0161) 2 31 55 37;
Fax: (00 37 2) 4 34 26 22; telex: 1 12 197/98

Cottbus
Gulbener Str. 24, O-7500 Cottbus
Tel: (00 37 959) 49 1-0; -1;
Fax: (00 37 959) 83 84 53; telex: 17 406

Dresden
Budapester Str. 5, O-8010 Dresden
Tel: (00 37 51) 4 85 24-74; -75;
Fax: (00 37 51) 4 85 24-76; telex: 2 431

Erfurt
Bahnhofstr. 37, O-5010 Erfurt
Tel: (00 37 61) 5 17 51; Fax: (00 37 61) 21 89 5;
telex: 61 417

Frankfurt/O
Halbe Stadt 7, O-1200 Frankfurt/O
Tel: (00 37 930) 31 14 15;
Fax: (00 37 930) 36 42 460; telex: 162 201

Gera
Puschkinplatz 7, O-6500 Gera
Tel: (00 37 970) 22 77 1;
Fax: (00 37 970) 24 07 0; telex: 58 283

Halle
Hochhaus 013, Postfach 155, O-4010 Halle
Tel: (00 37 46) 62 70; Fax: (00 37 46) 62 72 88;
telex: 4 514

Chemnitz
Neefestr. 119, O-9044 Chemnitz
Tel: (00 37 71) 36 79 0;
Fax: (00 37 71) 36 79 392; telex: 7 272

Leipzig
Friedrich-Engels-Platz 5, O-7010 Leipzig
Tel: (00 37 941) 21 72 0;
Fax: (00 37 941) 20 93 80; telex: 5 12 468

Magdeburg
Otto-v.-Guericke-Str. 27-28; O-3010 Magdeburg
Tel: (00 37 91) 37 90; Fax: (00 37 91) 32 91 2;
telex: 8 446

Neubrandenburg
Trockener Weg 7; O-2000 Neubrandenburg
Tel: (00 37 990) 66 50; Fax: (00 37 990) 42 09 0;
telex: 33 192

Potsdam
Am Bürohochhaus 2, O-1581 Potsdam
Tel: (00 37 23) 49 91; (030) 80 25 062
Fax; (030) 80 25 062 telex: 15 563

Rostock
Wilhelm-Külz-Platz 2, O-2500 Rostock
Tel: (00 37 81) 38 55 00; 38 50;
Fax: (00 37 81) 38 55 08

Schwerin
Karl-Marx-Str. 18, O-2750 Schwerin
Tel: (00 37 984) 35 70; Fax: (00 37 984) 35 74 16;
telex: 32 216

Suhl
Hölderlinstr. 1, O-6016 Suhl
Tel: (00 37 966) 60 20 3

The above information on the Treuhand has been culled from a variety of sources including the Treuhand itself and the "European Initiative for Eastern Germany", an organization of four major European banks which aims to promote investment in the new *Länder*. For further information, contact the main office in Frankfurt/Main, tel: (069) 13 62 26 36; Fax: (069) 13 62 20 08.

Ilka Eßmüller

How the Treuhand is Organized

President: Birgit Breuel

Economic Issues
Contacts to Federal and
Länder Governments
International Relations

Company Planning
Communication / Media
Legal questions
Auditing

Division 1

Construction of heavy machinery / plant
Machine tool manufacture
Special machinery

Administration and control of holdings
Examination of company concepts

Division 2

Optics / ceramics / precision instruments
Construction of vehicles
Coastal industries
Transportation

Reorganization *(Sanierung)*

Division 3

Agriculture / forestry
Mining
Food, beverages / tobacco

Administration
Organization / EDP

Division 4

Electrical engineering / electronics
Timber / paper / service sector
15 local offices / privatization issues

GPH (charged with privatization of
wholesalers / retailers)

Division 5

Iron / steel industry
Nonferrous-metal industry
Building industry
Hotels and guest houses
Financial assets
"THA Liegenschaften GmbH"
(in charge of THA real estate)
Expert group "Altlasten" (contamin. sites)

Division 6

Municipal assets
Water management
Energy
Chemical, textile, clothing and
leather industries
Special assets

Personnel

Personnel THA
Personnel subsidiaries
Labour and social affairs

Financial questions

Finance planning and control
Company financing
Financial statements and guarantees
Accounting / budget

Source: Federal Office of Foreign Trade Information

Germany is, perhaps, the one property market in the world which has yet to be affected by the world economic downturn and the question remains as to how long its strength can continue. Some feel that the recent tax increases to help finance the reconstruction of eastern Germany and contributions to the Gulf War (in effect as from 1 July 1991) could mark the beginning of a cooling down period for the German market. However, interest in German real estate from both domestic and international sources has never been stronger.

Berlin is a city which interests everyone but the market is a long way from settling down and clear investment patterns have yet to emerge. Other eastern German cities such as Leipzig and Dresden, although some way behind Berlin in terms of available infrastructure, are in a similar situation.

Frankfurt is still a favourite amongst many investors and continues to enjoy its status as the financial capital of the united Germany. Its position will be reinforced still further if the planned European central bank locates in the city. Certainly, there were a number of major investment transactions recorded in Frankfurt in early 1991 with the Japanese Kowa group buying the Fürstenhof for a reported figure of DM 450 million, clients of Nomura buying a majority share-holding in the Messeturm and Deutsche Bank taking over the new BfG (Bank für Gemeinwirtschaft) building on the Mainzer Landstraße. Both these latter deals were for buildings worth in excess of DM 1 billion on completion which indicates the level of confidence in the market.

Strangely enough, however, it is Hamburg which comes close to the top of most investors' shopping lists as the city with a sound economic structure as well as the "gateway to the east" following the opening-up of Eastern Europe.

Düsseldorf is a city recently favoured by French and Swedish investors, in particular, and certainly as capital of the resurgent Ruhr region looks to have a prosperous future. There are, however, worries about the amount of decentralized office accommodation which will be coming on the market over the next two to three years and which could well dampen rental growth.

The market in Munich is still adjusting to the effects of unification and the city's place in the future economic order in Germany. There is a suspicion that investment prices may have peaked and the effects of the new airport are far from clear. Prices remain high, however, and there is still a strong demand for any good quality real estate which comes on to the market.

Towns and cities such as Hanover, Kassel and even Nuremberg may recover much of their previous importance due to the opening of the east. Of all main centres within the Federal Republic, Bonn, with its recently booming property market, is the only obvious potential loser.

Investment yields for prime properties are similar throughout the country with prime office and retail investments fetching prices of between 4.25% and 4.5% whilst exceptional properties often make even better prices. The agents give as examples the sale of the Chase Bank building in Frankfurt in the summer of 1990 and their recent sale of an investment owned by Securitas-Gilde in Hamburg.

We can also report that the investment market is becoming far more analytical in its approach to reversionary properties, in particular, and internal rate of return calculations are a valid marketing tool for most types of property.

The domestic institutional investment market remains strong although the major open-ended funds are not as liquid as in previous years owing to the relatively high level of interest rates which attracts money into alternative investments. Interestingly enough, there is presently only limited interest amongst German institutions for investment in real estate abroad – although this may well change with the EC single market legislation – and the agents point out that the recent well-publicized purchases in London have been made by private German investors.

Foreign interest in Germany is growing and UK and Dutch investors and developers have been joined by increasing interest from the French as well as Swedish purchasers. A number of Swedish property companies have experienced problems over the last few months but the more soundly based companies and institutions are still strongly in the market. The Japanese are showing increasing interest in the country and have just started to invest significant sums of money, and there is strong interest among US development companies, although few major purchases have been announced. A growing number of European property investment funds are also targeting the German market, such as German City Estates Fund sponsored by London and Edinburgh Trust and SPP, and West German Property Fund sponsored by Enskilda Fondkommission. In addition, the Pan European Property Unit Trust Fund has been established for some years and has a DM 300 million portfolio of properties.

The office side shows strong rental growth in nearly every major city. Prime rentals in Frankfurt have moved from DM 75 per sq metre to DM 90 per sq metre over the last 12 months although the market at this level is relatively "thin".

Property in Berlin is almost impossible to value, according to the agents, as no prime buildings are available and smaller suites of offices around the Kurfürstendamm are being put on the market at up to DM 80 to DM 100 per sq metre. The market there is expected to remain tight, one reason being that many new developments are on hold until planning authorities have finalized a blueprint for the city. At the same time, construction costs in Berlin seem to be rising more quickly than in other parts of Germany.

Prime rents in Hamburg are now between DM 40 and DM 45 per sq metre and a similar figure can be applied to prime accommodation in Düsseldorf around the Königsallee. Top rents in Munich are now in excess of DM 60 per sq metre but the agents point out that this applies only to exceptional buildings in downtown locations and that a more normal figure is between DM 25 and DM 35 per sq metre.

Most retailers in Germany went through an exceptionally good trading year in 1990 and experienced record turnovers. Many German retailers are, however, preoccupied with expansion into the new *Länder* and this has affected their international expansion rather than plans for other parts of Germany.

The economic conditions in Germany have, understandably, attracted foreign retailers and a number of "household names" have aggressive plans for expansion. The German marketplace is, however, exceptionally competitive and has proved difficult for foreign retailers, especially from the UK, to enter in the past.

Prime retail rentals do not vary significantly throughout the country although highest rents are to be found in cities like Munich and Cologne at levels of DM 400 per sq metre and above for smaller units whereas other major centres such as Frankfurt, Berlin, Düsseldorf and Hamburg are in a range of DM 300 to DM 350 per sq metre.

One aspect of which many investors complain, particularly those new to the market, is the lack of product. In the new *Länder* companies and space are becoming available for a variety of reasons. However, the uncertainties regarding property ownership are still apparent and in some cases holding up investment. Moreover, the quality of the property will have to be upgraded significantly before it meets western standards. It remains a valid comment for the western part of the country that there is less turnover of property than in many other countries. The reasons for this are varied and include a high incidence of owner occupation – 44% of all office buildings are owner occupied – an unwillingness amongst many institutional investors to trade properties within their portfolios and an increasing worry amongst private investors that too frequent trading could lead to the loss of significant tax advantages.

As to speculative building in our experience, the following can be taken as realistic price guides, based upon current tender figures:

Central area offices: DM 2,500 to DM 3,000   per sq metre
Decentralized offices: DM 1,600 to DM 2,200   per sq metre
Warehousing: DM 1,000 to DM 1,100   per sq metre

To these figures should be added professional fees and licences at around 15% together with *Mehrwertsteuer* (value-added tax) at 14%. These figures are, of course, indicative of typical buildings and will vary from city to city according to the capacity of the local construction industry and the difficulty of individual sites as well as standards of finish required by market conditions.

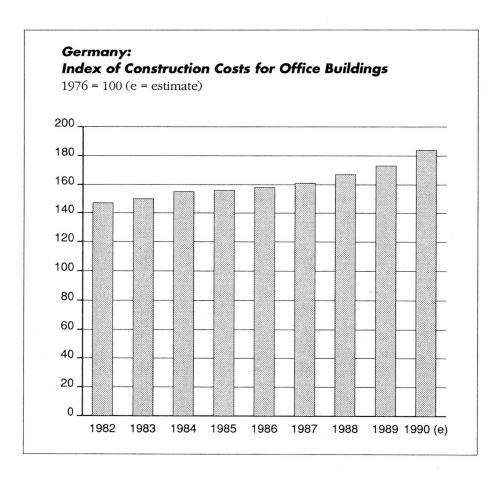

Germany:
Index of Construction Costs for Office Buildings
1976 = 100 (e = estimate)

Despite the weight of money looking to enter the market, yields have changed only at the margin over the last 12 months. Yield structures can be summarized as follows:

Offices	1. Prime central area	4.25% to 5%
	2. Other central locations	5% to 5.5%
	3. Decentralized	5.25% to 6.5%
Retail	1. Prime central area	4.25% to 4.75%
	2. Other central locations	4.75% to 5.5%
	3. Secondary	5.5% to 6.5%
	4. Retail warehousing	6.5% to 7.5%
Warehousing	1. Modern and well located	7% to 8.5%
	2. Secondary	8.5% to 12%+

As far as the future is concerned, there seems no limit to the amount of foreign money seeking to be invested in the German market and, with the opening-up of Eastern Europe and the medium term opportunities for investment in what had been the East Bloc countries, it is even probable that these sums will continue to be invested.

An Example of Market Development: Frankfurt

Frankfurt is still at the top of many investors' requirement lists. It is, of course, primarily known as Germany's financial capital and is generally regarded as the world's fourth most important banking city after New York, Tokyo and London. There are now around 400 banks in Frankfurt, of which 255 are foreign, and the city also houses the most important stock exchange in Germany. The decision by the federal government to retain the Bundesbank in Frankfurt looks to have secured the long term future of the city in this role and there is now a strong possibility that the proposed new European central bank will be located in Germany, in which case Frankfurt would be a natural location.

Frankfurt is, however, more than a financial capital. Although it is a small city with a population of 628,000, it acts as the effective regional centre for the prosperous Rhine-Main conurbation which has a population in excess of two million inhabitants. The city and its surrounding area also have a significant industrial base including major employers such as Hoechst Chemicals at Höchst and Opel, the German branch of General Motors, which is based at Rüsselsheim.

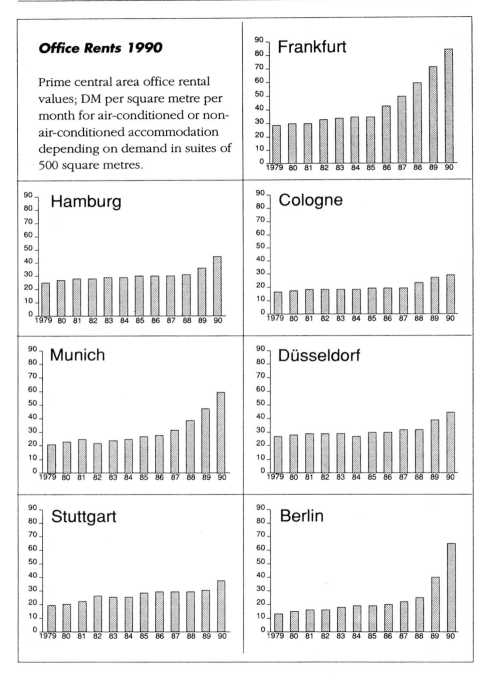

Office Rents 1990

Prime central area office rental values; DM per square metre per month for air-conditioned or non-air-conditioned accommodation depending on demand in suites of 500 square metres.

Frankfurt

Hamburg

Cologne

Munich

Düsseldorf

Stuttgart

Berlin

Frankfurt is also, of course, a major trade fair and exhibition centre as well as one of the major European communication points with an important international airport.

The Office Market. The Frankfurt office market has seen dramatic fluctuations over the last twenty years. Until the early Seventies, office rentals in Frankfurt had enjoyed virtually unbroken growth since the end of the Second World War but the economic boom in 1971 and 1972 led to an oversupply coming onto the market which demand could not have absorbed even in the most buoyant economic conditions. In the early years of the oil crises, however, economic conditions were anything but buoyant and a vast oversupply of office accommodation was created so that in the mid-Seventies Frankfurt achieved a reputation as having the most oversupply of office accommodation – in excess of 400,000 sq metres against an annual take-up which, even in the best years, had scarcely exceeded 100,000 sq metres. As a result, a number of major buildings were left in a semi-completed state as financing banks withdrew their loan support.

The supply of offices was eventually up but not before rental values had fallen significantly from their levels in 1973 and 1974. Indeed, it was not until the early Eighties that rentals achieved within the main banking area climbed through their earlier peak of DM 30 per sq metre. Frankfurt was, of course, not alone in this trend which was repeated in most other German cities and elsewhere throughout the world's main office centres.

During the early Eighties, rental growth throughout the city continued at a relatively modest pace, matching the low levels of inflation which have been a feature of the German economy, and prime rents within the banking area had increased only to around DM 35 per sq metre by the mid-Eighties. Since most of the central area of Frankfurt had been rebuilt following almost complete devastation in the Second World War, the majority of existing buildings were viewed by their owners as having a higher worth as created investments, notwithstanding their lack of modern facilities, rather than as sites capable of profitable redevelopment. As such, relatively few properties came onto the market for redevelopment purposes and the supply of new accommodation within the central area of the city came almost to a standstill. This problem was intensified by the policies of many of the German banks and insurance companies which held properties for future development for their own purposes, as well as by restrictive policies adopted by the Frankfurt municipal authorities.

The expansion of demand from the banking and financial services industries from around 1985 onward therefore found Frankfurt severely lacking in modern accommodation.

The resultant boom was, of course, largely predictable and prime central rentals have moved from around DM 35 per sq metre to a general level of DM 70 to DM 75 per sq metre with isolated lettings reaching up to DM 85 to DM 90 per sq metre. It is, moreover, interesting to note that the main demand during this period has come from the domestic banking organizations and that rentals of the highest levels have been paid by the major German banks as well as by international concerns seeking prestige accommodation within the city centre. The total take-up figure for all types of office accommodation in 1990 was around 250,000 sq metres and according to Weatherall's records the total supply of office accommodation available for letting in 1991 is presently under 200,000 sq metres in the whole of Frankfurt. Weatherall apportion this as follows:

Banking area/Westend: 97,000 sq metres
City: 6,400 sq metres
West: 12,200 sq metres
Eschborn: 36,000 sq metres
Niederrad: 55,200 sq metres

These figures include a substantial proportion of older office accommodation or poorly located buildings which may remain vacant for a considerable period of time but taken against the official estimate of the total stock of office accommodation in Frankfurt at around eight million sq metres, the vacancy rate realistically represents 2.5%. At present, Frankfurt has about 300,000 sq metres of new accommodation either under construction or at an advanced planning stage and over one million sq metres in planning although much of this will not be available until the mid- to late Nineties. Since a significant proportion of this space can be expected to be taken up for owner occupation, the letting market is likely to remain tight at least until 1994/5 and the situation will be particularly acute in central business district locations. Although demand at the highest rental levels is not as strong as some reports would have the market believe, Weatheralls suggest from their tenants' enquiries that a high quality building in a main banking address would probably let today for between DM 90 and DM 100 per sq metre but point out that, as no such building exists, this is a purely subjective view.

Certainly, travelling around Frankfurt the number of tower cranes point to a mass of building activity but the majority of these schemes are for owner occupation. There are, however, a number of new projects coming onto the market in prime downtown locations which will undoubtedly set new rental levels for the city. These include schemes by MEPC, Pan European as well as the recently acquired Kowa building and there will be space to let in new tower schemes under construction for DG-Bank and Deutsche Bank/BfG.

Retail Market. The retail market has also performed strongly in Frankfurt and according to Weatheralls the affluence of the city has now been recognized not only by domestic retailing groups but also by international concerns wanting to either establish themselves or expand their representation within the Federal Republic. Works of improvement by the Frankfurt city government have had a major effect upon the appearance of the central area of the city and the Goethe-straße, for instance, is now one of the most sought-after fashion retailing addresses in the country. Recent important retail acquisitions by Weatheralls on behalf of French retailer Hermes and American jeweller Tiffany's prove the point. Other important transactions secured by the agents in the recent past include a large shop for American fashion retailer Esprit in Steinweg.

Prime rents in the Goethestraße are now up to DM 300 per sq metre or marginally above and smaller units on high-turnover locations such as the Zeil can be expected to reach up to DM 400 per sq metre.

The Investment Market. Over the last few years, Frankfurt has seen a number of spectacular investment and development transactions but these have been eclipsed by a number of the deals concluded during the latter part of 1990.

Strong rental growth in the office and retail sectors coupled with shortages of supply and a realization that Frankfurt was unlikely to "lose out" to Berlin following unification meant that Frankfurt has been a sought-after location both by German and international investor and developer groups. German funds have continued to be strongly in the market although a number of the open-ended funds have found their liquidity levels reduced by high returns available to the smaller investors from other investment media. Dutch, Swedish, French and American groups have also been active in the marketplace and the Japanese, after a long period of study, have now moved into the scene with a number of spectacular purchases. There is also increasing interest from the UK, both from investors and property companies.

The sale by Chase Bank of their former headquarters building on Taunus-anlage in early autumn 1990 at a spectacular price reported to be around DM 200 million marked an important shift forward and, interestingly, this property was acquired for refurbishment by a German open-ended fund, DGI Deutsche Grund-besitz Investment. On current market rentals this purchase analyzed at a yield of around 4%.

The Chase Bank sale was followed around the year end by the announcement of the purchase of Fürstenhof by the Japanese Kowa group for a reported price of around DM 450 million. This scheme is being developed by private investor Dr. Schneider and comprises some 15,000 sq metres of office accommodation together with retail and banking hall facilities. It was concluded on a "turnkey basis" for completion in 1992 and was reportedly secured without rental guarantees.

At the same time, Nomura put together a group of Japanese investors who purchased into the Messeturm development being undertaken by Tishman Speyer, Kajima and Citibank and Deutsche Bank bought another 60,000 sq metre tower under construction from the troubled Bank für Gemeinwirtschaft next door to their own headquarters on the Mainzer Landstraße. Both these properties will have a value on completion in excess of DM 1 billion.

Finally, the Industrial Bank of Japan were selected as developers for the proposed new Japanese Centre in the heart of the banking area at the corner of Neue Mainzer Straße and Große Gallusstraße.

Smaller investment transactions included the sale of the Legal & General portfolio which comprised a number of smaller retail and office investments to Schroders International Property Fund at a reported price of around DM 60 million.

Weatheralls point out that it became increasingly difficult to place firm figures of value on prime real estate but, as a guide, suggest that yields are now between 4% and 4.5% for prime opportunities but note that special locations might well command figures above these levels, particularly if an owner-occupier is involved.

The above report on the German market is optimistic; we have been watching the ups and downs of the German market over the past two decades and reckon that the market is generally in better shape than we have seen it at any time in the past. There are a number of "cowboy" elements as there inevitably are in any boom market, but first class buying opportunities exist for prudent investors and developers alike.

The above information has been supplied by Weatherall Green & Smith, Chartered Surveyors, Frankfurt. For further information, contact Christopher Bull-Diamond at (069) 273 00 00.

Taxation in Germany

Germany is generally regarded as a high tax country, certainly in terms of the tax rates and the variety of taxes imposed on corporate business enterprises. This chapter summarizes the main features of the German corporate and personal tax systems as they are likely to impact a non-resident who is considering:
a. The establishment of a German business venture
or
b. Taking up residence in Germany.

The information provided is, of necessity, more of a general nature, covering some of the broader issues which the non-resident should consider before an investment decision is taken. It is based, unless otherwise indicated, on the rules in effect on 1 January 1991. The taxation system which applied in the "old" Federal Republic now applies throughout united Germany, but there have been proposals, for example, that the tax system in the five new *Länder* should be modified to incorporate now at least some of the tax relief measures which are expected to be introduced in 1993 as part of the proposed business tax reform. The unification of Germany and the financing of German unity have placed extra demands on the Finance Ministry and, at the time of writing, it is still not clear whether the proposals published up to now will be implemented unchanged. For this reason, local advisers should be consulted before any decision in a specific investment situation is taken.

1. Corporate Taxation

German companies are subject to German tax on their worldwide income, while non-resident companies are subject to German tax only on their income from German sources. A resident company is defined as one which has either its seat **or** place of management in Germany. If a resident company receives income from foreign sources, this is either:
a. Subject to German tax with a tax credit being granted for the foreign income tax paid.

or

b. Exempt from German tax.

Exemption from German tax generally applies under existing tax treaties to income from foreign (non-German) branch operations or to dividends from a shareholding of 10% or more in a foreign company.

There are two main types of legal entity which are used in Germany, the *Aktiengesellschaft,* commonly referred to as "AG" and the *Gesellschaft mit beschränkter Haftung,* commonly referred to as "GmbH". The GmbH form is adopted by the vast majority of foreign enterprises for their German operations if they decide to carry these on within a German legal vehicle. If the non-resident decides to carry out his operations directly, without a German legal vehicle, he may choose the branch format. This is normally adopted in special situations where, for example, substantial initial losses are anticipated and the country of the head office offers the possibility to offset German branch losses immediately against the taxable income of the head office or where the direct support or reputation of the head office is likely to be a major factor in the commercial success of the German operations. Banking is perhaps the best example of this latter situation. A foreign company is subject to German tax on business income from German sources only if it maintains a permanent establishment (branch office) in Germany.

Types of Tax on Corporate Income. Two types of tax are imposed in Germany on corporate income:
a. Corporation profits tax *(Körperschaftsteuer).*
and
b. Trade tax on income *(Gewerbeertragsteuer).*

Corporation profits tax is a federal tax and levied at the following rates:
- 36% on taxable income of resident companies to the extent it is distributed to shareholders.
- 50% on the undistributed taxable income of resident companies.
- 46% on the taxable income of non-resident companies, irrespective of whether or not it is distributed.

The corporation profits tax follows the imputation tax system, with a full tax credit being granted to a resident shareholder, whether a company or a natural person, for the full amount of the corporation profits tax attached to the dividend distribution. A non-resident is generally not entitled to the German imputation tax credit. If, however, a German branch of a non-resident entity receives dividend income from a German company, a tax credit is granted.

The revenue from the trade tax on income (and capital) flows to the municipalities. The tax rate is calculated by applying to the 5% basic rate (which applies Germany-wide) the municipal factors which are set each year by the different municipalities in which the business operates. Because these factors generally vary between 300% and 500% and because the trade tax itself is a deductible expense in arriving at taxable income for trade tax purposes, the effective tax rates vary between about 13% and 20%. Trade tax is a deductible expense for corporation profits tax purposes. The corporation profits tax payable in 1991 and 1992 is to be increased by a temporary surcharge of 3.75% in each year. Thus, for example, the impact in the tax rate for distributions is effectively 1.35%. The surcharge is imposed outside the imputation tax system, so that a resident shareholder receives *no* tax credit for the surcharge paid on dividends received.

An example showing in simplified form a comparison of the taxes payable by a branch of a foreign company and by a German resident company is provided in Table 1. This example also reflects the impact of German withholding tax.

Withholding tax is not a separate tax but rather a different form of collection of tax (as its name implies, by withholding of tax at source). Withholding tax on dividend distributions is therefore in effect the collection of tax from

Simplified Comparison of German Corporate Income Taxes Payable by a Branch or Subsidiary of a Foreign Company

	Branch	Subsidiary
Profit before tax	1,000	1,000
Trade tax on income (Frankfurt rate)	194	194
Profit after trade income tax	806	806
Corporation profits tax 46% – Branch	371	
50% – Subsidiary (profits retained)		403
Income after (initial) corporation profits tax	435	403
Corporation profits tax refund on distribution (14/50)	0	(113)
Gross dividend	516	
Dividend withholding tax assumed at 15%[1]		77
Net amount to head office/ parent company	435	43
Effective tax rate[2]	56.5%	56.1%

1 Germany has recently renegotiated a number of tax treaties with important trading partners to reduce (to 10%) the rate of dividend withholding tax. The rate is expected to be reduced further to 5% from 1992 onward as a result of EC initiatives.

2 The corporation profits tax payable in 1991 and 1992 is to be increased by a temporary surcharge of 3.75% in each year. Because the surcharge is a non-deductible business expense, it has a greater impact on the corporation profits tax payable than would appear at first sight. In the comparison above, the tax payable by a company which distributes all of its taxable income is increased from 290 (403 less 113) to 309 and the effective tax rate is increased to 57.8% as compared to 57.9% in the case of a branch.

the recipient of the income. In comparing the German taxes payable by a branch and a subsidiary company, however, it is necessary to reflect the withholding tax, because it is payable on dividend distributions by a German company to its foreign parent but not on profits remitted by a German branch to its foreign head office. The normal rate of withholding tax is 25%, and it is deductible at source from dividend, royalty and certain interest payments, although not from interest on straightforward loans. The withholding tax rate on payments to non-residents is reduced, in many instances to nil, under the terms of Germany's tax treaties with foreign countries.

Determination of Taxable Income. The starting point for the determination of taxable income is the profit for the year as shown in the corporate entity's accounts prepared for tax purposes. Since the tax accounts in general correspond with the statutory financial statements, any valuation options exercised in the latter will also have an effect in the taxation area.

No distinction is made between capital and revenue gains and losses, but it is possible to postpone the taxation of all or part of the gain on the sale of certain fixed assets where the gain is offset against the cost of certain replacement items.

In valuing assets and liabilities, the so-called "imparity" rule applies; this means that provision for unrealized losses is required, while gains will only be recognized when they have been realized.

Business expenses deducted in the commercial financial statements are generally deductible for tax purposes unless there is a specific requirement under the tax law that these should be added back. Among the more important of these for corporation profits tax purposes are corporation profits tax itself and net assets tax, and the addback of 20% of entertaining expenses. The temporary 3.75% surcharge to be imposed in 1991 and 1992 will also fall into this category. Perhaps the most important item from the point of view of the non-resident investor is the addback which is required for so-called "hidden distributions of profits".

A hidden distribution of profits is assumed when, in dealings between a German company and its (resident or non-resident parent or affiliates) transactions are not carried out on an arm's length basis, with the result that the taxable income in Germany is (deemed to be) understated. Examples of "hidden distributions" are excessive charges from a parent or affiliate in respect of goods sold or services rendered to the German company, sales by the German company to the parent or affiliate at prices below arm's length terms, excessive royalty or interest payments by the German company, etc. The tax implications on the assumption of a hidden distribution of profits can be severe. In the worst case, the tax payable on the disallowed amount may exceed the amount of the "dividend" itself. It is, however, possible to take steps to ensure that penal tax implications are alleviated. The tax authorities have published guidelines on the principles which they believe should be followed in determining whether transactions have been concluded on an arm's length basis.

Intercompany Charges. Transactions between a German company and its domestic or foreign parent or affiliate are normally subjected to a careful scrutiny by the tax authorities. This is particularly the case where a non-resident parent or affiliate is concerned, because the tax administration is keen to ensure that the amount of income subject to German tax has not been reduced artificially. Such scrutiny takes place during the course of tax audits which are carried out by the German tax administration at regular (three to five year) intervals. These tax audits involve a detailed review of the intercompany transactions during the period covered by the tax audit, with the result that it is not unusual for audits to last three months or more. In principle, all transactions between members of a group which are accepted as being on an arm's length basis will be recognized for tax purposes.

Debt/Equity Rules. The fact that interest paid is per se a deductible expense and not normally subject to withholding tax, even if paid abroad, combined with the high rates of German corporate taxation, has increasingly led foreign parent companies to consider the debt/equity mix used to finance their German operations. Aware of this, the German tax administration has issued a decree in which it expresses the view that a company will be regarded as "under-capitalized" if its shareholders' equity at the year end is less than 10% of the German balance sheet total. If this is the case, and the company has received loans from affiliates, a portion of these loans will be regarded as "hidden capital", with the result that interest payments on such amounts are reconstituted as hidden distributions of profit, with the tax implications described above. The tax courts have not been very supportive up to now of the tax administration's views, and attempts by the government over the past ten years to draft more restrictive legislation have so far been unsuccessful.

Losses. For corporation profits tax purposes, losses must first be carried back and offset against taxable income of the previous two years. The total amount of the loss carryback for any one year is limited to DM 10 million, and the carryback and offset is restricted to taxable income of preceding years which has not yet been distributed. (Effectively this means that the loss carryback leads to a refund of the tax which would otherwise have been levied at the 50% (in earlier years 56%) retention rate rather than the 36% distribution rate). Any unutilized balance of losses may be carried forward for corporation profits tax purposes without limit. For trade tax purposes, tax losses may be carried forward, but not carried back.

Group Relief. Under the German *Organschaft* concept, it is possible to pool the profits or losses of German group companies, both for corporation profits tax and for trade income tax purposes, provided certain conditions are fulfilled. The controlling (German) group company must hold more than 50% of the shares of the German subsidiary company and in addition exercise organizational and economic control over the German subsidiaries. In addition, a written profit and loss pooling agreement for a period of at least five years is required for the pooling to be effective for corporation profits tax purposes.

Investment Incentives. Germany offers a number of regional and industry incentives designed to favour depressed areas and industries with long-term structural difficulties. The incentives take the form of accelerated depreciation or cash investment grants. The reunification of Germany is leading to the phasing-out of a number of incentives which have been in place for many years (in Berlin and along what was the zonal border with East Germany), while new incentives have been introduced, particularly in eastern Germany. These changes, which are in part still under discussion, make it difficult to offer meaningful comments in this chapter, so that detailed information based on the location of the proposed investment and the industry involved should be sought on a case-by-case basis.

Taxable Income for Trade Tax Purposes. The starting point for the determination of taxable income for trade tax purposes is the income for corporation profits tax purposes. Certain adjustments are required under the trade tax law, the most important addacks being:

a. One half of the interest on long-term loans, such as loans for the purposes of extending or expanding the business operations or where the loan is for a period in excess of 12 months.

b. One half of the amount of rental payments for moveable assets unless the lessor is subject to trade tax on the rental receipt.

Other Taxes. These can be divided into two main groups, namely taxes on capital and transactions taxes. The first category includes net assets tax, a tax which is imposed at the rate of 0.6% on 75% of the taxable business net assets over DM 125,000 yearly. Trade capital tax also falls under this heading and is imposed at a Germany-wide basic rate of 0.2%, increased, as for trade income tax, by the individual municipal factors to effective rates of between 0.6% and 1.0% per annum. The taxable assets for trade tax purposes are determined on a different basis than for net assets tax purposes. Thus, one half of the long-term loans is, for example, not deductible as a liability in arriving at taxable net assets for trade tax purposes. The most important of the transactions taxes is the value-added tax, which is levied at a standard rate of 14% on the proceeds of sales and services effected in Germany. Certain transactions are subject to tax at a reduced 7% rate. The tax is a classical value-added tax system, so that business enterprises are entitled to offset against their value-added tax payable the amount of tax charged to them by their suppliers or assessed on imports.

Other important transaction taxes are the 1% capital transactions tax, which is imposed on capital introduced into a business by its shareholders and the real estate acquisition tax, which is levied at the rate of 2% on transactions involving the transfer of real estate, including the acquisition of all the shares in a company which owns real estate. Capital transactions tax is planned to be eliminated from 1 January 1992 onward.

2. Personal Taxation

Resident individuals are subjected to German tax on their worldwide income. Generally an individual is deemed to be a resident if he is physically present in Germany for more than six months or if he has accommodation at his disposal under circumstances which indicate that he intends to retain and use it (longer rental contract). The tax year is the calendar year, and taxable income is based on income received during the year. If an individual is a resident for only part of the year, he will be taxed only on the income received during the period of residence.

Married persons resident in Germany may choose to be assessed jointly or separately, whichever is more favourable to them. If assessed jointly, they will pay tax equivalent to twice the tax payable at the basic rate on one half of their combined income.

An individual (or married couple) who received income from employment and whose gross annual income after deduction of income-connected expenses exceeds DM 27,000 (DM 54,000 for a married couple on joint assessment) must file an annual income tax return. A person (or married couple) with incomes of less than these amounts need generally only file a return if he is in receipt of income exceeding DM 800 from which no salary tax has been deducted or if he received dividend income from which withholding tax has been deducted.

Gains on the sale of privately owned land are exempt from taxation if the holding period exceeds two years. Gains on the sale of other assets, primarily gains on the sale of securities, are exempt if the holding period exceeds six months.

Church tax is payable by all members of the Roman Catholic, Jewish or Protestant faith. The rate varies according to district and generally amounts to between 8% and 9% of the income tax payable. Church tax is collected by the tax office in the same manner as and together with German income taxes. A foreign national coming to Germany will not be required to pay this tax if he ensures that, when registering with the local authorities, no religious affiliation is entered in the registration record or on his wage tax card.

German Income Tax Payable on Gross Income for 1991 (in DM)

Gross income	Single person	Married couple assessed jointly	Married couple 2 children
50,000	9,351	5,862	4,524
75,000	17,824	12,200	10,624
100,000	28,156	19,320	17,514
150,000	53,659	36,382	34,118
200,000	80,161	57,244	54,518
250,000	106,663	81,902	78,720
300,000	133,165	108,406	105,200
400,000	186,169	161,410	158,204
500,000	239,174	214,414	211,208

The above calculations reflect standard deductions for employees as follows:

	1991
single	5,618
married	9,236
married, one child	12,260
married, two children	15,284
married, three children	18,308

In arriving at taxable income, a number of deductions are permitted, mainly under the heading of expenses incurred in acquiring, securing and obtaining income – so-called income-related expenses – and special expenses, which include insurance or social security contributions, education allowance of children attending school away from home, fees for tax consultation, etc. Table 2 shows the German income tax payable on gross compensation at various income levels.

The income tax payable in 1991 and 1992 is to be increased by a temporary surcharge. The surcharge will apply between 1 July 1991 and 30 June 1992 and will be at a rate of 7.5%. Effectively, this means that the income tax payable for the calendar years 1991 and 1992 will be increased by 3.75% in each year.

The above information has been provided by Price Waterhouse, Frankfurt. For further information, contact Geoffrey S. Twinem at (069) 15 20 40.

Who Gets What – Compensation for German Managers

The data provided has been taken from the Kienbaum compensation survey of top, senior and middle management. It is based on information provided by 538 companies on a total of 4,435 executives.

What follows is a breakdown of the 538 companies by sales turnover and number of employees:

Turnover in DM	No. of Companies
Below 15 million	60
15 to 30 million	69
30 to 150 million	204
150 to 300 million	78
300 to 750 million	82
Above 750 million	45
Total	538

No. of Employees	No. of Companies
Under 100	85
100 to 250	154
250 to 1,000	166
1,000 to 5,000	98
Over 5,000	35
Total	538

Background

The traditional approach to compensation in Germany was to pay base salaries with few or no variable extras in order to keep salary levels within a stable framework.

Since the Seventies, this approach has changed considerably and more flexible compensation policies have been introduced to deal with increasing personnel costs. Compensation packages of executives show greater flexibility than do those of non-managerial employees. Companies are realizing that executives are not so much cost factors as profit producers, and the efforts of managers to increase company profits are now being recognized and rewarded in the form of incentive and bonus payments.

The compensation of executives in Germany was originally based on the often strongly defended premise that money cannot motivate. However, this premise is rather narrow – the results of a representative survey conducted by the EMNID Institute show that better pay is the primary factor in getting employees, even top managers, to work harder. The level of compensation in Germany is now seen as an indicator of the company's esteem for the manager and his performance, and a tailor-made compensation package gives a company the opportunity to motivate its executives. This compensation policy turnabout has been influenced by both consultancies and multinational companies.

Factors Influencing Compensation

Salary structures in Germany are influenced by a variety of factors:

- As in most countries, the size of the company is the primary and most important determinant of salary levels. The larger the company (measured by turnover, number of employees or balance sheet total), the greater the compensation the executives receive. For senior management in companies with high annual turnover, salaries may be 46% higher than for senior management in companies with lower annual turnover. Based on the number of employees, this company-to-company difference in senior management salaries is 42%. The reasoning behind this considerable pay discrepancy is that senior managers in large companies are supposed to carry greater responsibility and have more complex and demanding jobs than their counterparts in smaller companies. It can also be argued, however, that senior managers in small and medium-sized companies have more direct responsibility (because structures are less rigid) and have to be more flexible.

- Company performance and earnings are another major determinant of compensation, particularly in the case of managing directors (but senior and middle managers are also affected). The managing director of a company with below industry-average earnings receives about 25% less than his counterpart in a company showing average performance, while the managing director of a company with above-average earnings may earn 10% more.

On the senior and middle management level, total pay tends to deviate from the average by about 5% depending on whether company earnings are better or worse than average.

- Factors such as age, performance, education etc. do not necessarily influence the compensation of any given individual; they have been observed as contributing to trends which apply, on average, to a number of companies.

- Although higher education has some impact on starting salaries and certainly on chances of promotion, experience plays a greater role in determining pay. Average salaries in a particular function are usually achieved at 46 years of age.

- Interestingly enough, executive salaries do not vary significantly from industry to industry. Within a given industrial sector, however, there are compensation differences between manufacturing, trading and service companies. Manufacturing companies tend to pay higher salaries: about 2% above average.

- It is too soon to talk about salaries in eastern Germany. For the rest, factors such as geographical location, size of the community or the company's legal form are of little or no relevance to the salaries of executives.

Bonuses

Total compensation in Germany as outlined in the salary tables at the end of this chapter includes base salary – usually paid in 13 instalments and with a Christmas and/or vacation "allowance" added in – plus variable elements, i.e. bonuses.

Bonuses are an important tool in a company's compensation policy. They are intended to reward and motivate by relating company or individual performance to pay.

The payment and amount of variable compensation are, to a large extent, tied to the earnings situation of an individual company. Companies with below-average performance make fewer and smaller bonus payments. When company performance is good, bonuses can be very high. Bonuses for managing directors can vary by about 100%, depending on company earnings. They vary by 30% on the senior and 15% on the middle management levels.

It should be noted that share option schemes do not exist in Germany; at the present time, the government has no plans to introduce legislation which would make such schemes tax-attractive.

The following are average bonus payments made to executives in each function.

Function	Recipients %	Amount in DM
Managing Director	88	59,000
Personnel	72	27,000
Finance	70	25,000
Sales & Marketing	77	29,000
Manufacturing	73	29,000
Purchasing	60	23,000
Research & Development	80	27,000
EDP/IT[1]	71	24,000

1 Electronic Data Processing/Information Technology

Salary Administration

In Germany, job evaluation systems are not common, although they are implemented in some subsidiaries of multinational companies.

Salaries and salary structures are generally established by the prevailing market rate; a position as outlined in a job description is compared to similar or related positions and compensated accordingly. Only in large companies do salary structures sometimes develop.

As mentioned earlier, the payment of a 13th monthly "instalment" is common and generally included in the base annual salary.

Salary increases for executives are normally awarded once a year. The most common date for salary reviews is 1 January and 40% of all salary increases become effective on that date. Other common dates for salary reviews are 1 April (15%), 1 October, 1 March and 1 June (10% each). There is a clear relationship between salary increases and the age of the recipient. Younger employees normally receive above-average salary increases. Average salary increases are reached at age 40 or 45. Older managers receive below-average increases.

Salary increases for managers are based on collective bargaining agreements but are supplemented by an additional percentage for performance.

Benefits

Benefits are a very important element of the compensation package. German companies strictly separate salary and benefits.

Pension Schemes. Company-provided retirement benefits are the most important and most expensive of all benefits. Social security benefits are not sufficient to guarantee managers an adequate standard of living after retirement. Nowadays, approximately 65% of pre-retirement income is considered a sufficient retirement figure. However, the maximum social security pension and a reasonable amount of private pension can still leave a gap of approximately 30-50% in the desirable retirement income, depending on the salary level.

Companies have therefore recognized the need for additional retirement plans for their managers. These plans fall within normal company benefits. Fifteen years ago only 70% of all managers were covered under such a plan, compared with 85% today.

The incidence of private benefit plans is primarily dependent on the size of the company. Smaller companies still lag behind in this respect.

Company pension schemes represent the most popular type of retirement plan for management, especially in larger companies. Smaller companies tend to prefer direct insurance policies, since these require less company administration.

Company pension schemes typically provide for additional retirement income, as well as survivors' benefits – pensions for widows and orphans.

The percentage of retirement income from a company pension scheme depends on the manager's rank in the company hierarchy. While a managing director can count on about 50% of the final base salary after 25 years, senior managers usually receive a maximum of 40%, middle managers 35%.

Company Cars. The second most important benefit is the company car. While most firms reduced their car fleets substantially at the beginning of the last decade, the present number of employees with a company car is increasing rapidly. Currently, more than 50% of executives drive company cars. Cars are provided less because they are needed for business-related activities than because they are a tax-advantageous form of extra compensation.

The provision of company cars is partly dependent on the size of the company. Companies with up to 100 employees provide company cars more often (up to 60%) than companies with 1,000 to 5,000 employees (40% to 55%). However, in companies with more than 5,000 employees, 70% of the managers are granted a company car.

Other Benefits. Other benefits for managers include accident insurance, continued salary payments in case of temporary disability and company loans.

Annual vacation averages 30 working days. Both management and staff receive the same amount of paid vacation.

Compensation Adjustment for 1991

The survey data which follows was effective as of 1 May 1990. Executive salary increases for 1990-1991 are expected to be approximately 8% for managing directors and 6% for other levels of management. The figures in the compensation tables should therefore be increased accordingly to bring them approximately up to date.

Base Salaries by Function and Turnover (DM million)

(the amount given represents the median average of figures provided)

Function	Up to 15	15 to 30	30 to 150	150 to 300	300 to 1,500	Over 1,500
Managing Director	167,000	192,000	214,000	225,000	273,000	315,000
Personnel	89,000	91,000	113,000	127,000	144,000	175,000
Finance	94,000	106,000	126,000	133,000	151,000	189,000
Sales & Marketing	99,000	125,000	142,000	151,000	179,000	181,000
Manufacturing	107,000	115,000	134,000	157,000	184,000	195,000
Research & Development	(106,000)[1]	109,000	129,000	145,000	166,000	188,000
EDP/IT[2]	107,000	108,000	121,000	129,000	151,000	162,000

1 indicates a small sample
2 EDP/IT: Electronic Data Processing/Information Technology)

Total Compensation by Function and Turnover (DM million)

Function	Up to 15	15 to 30	30 to 150	150 to 300	300 to 1,500	Over 1,500
Managing Director	183,000	219,000	250,000	282,000	305,000	394,000
Personnel	93,000	104,000	122,000	136,000	156,000	195,000
Finance	99,000	115,000	137,000	142,000	160,000	206,000
Sales & Marketing	106,000	142,000	156,000	166,000	203,000	196,000
Manufacturing	109,000	124,000	140,000	162,000	203,000	208,000
Research & Development	(117,000)	114,000	142,000	153,000	183,000	190,000
EDP/IT	109,000	110,000	129,000	137,000	164,000	179,000

Base Salaries by Function and Number of Employees

Function	Up to 100	100 to 250	250 to 1,000	1,000 to 5,000	5,000 to 10,000	Over
Managing Director	184,000	216,000	223,000	219,000	286,000	347,000
Personnel	96,000	95,000	128,000	134,000	153,000	201,000
Finance	113,000	115,000	132,000	146,000	158,000	220,000
Sales & Marketing	112,000	137,000	144,000	170,000	173,000	185,000
Manufacturing	108,000	119,000	140,000	158,000	176,000	213,000
Research & Development	(108,000)	123,000	134,000	150,000	158,000	184,000
EDP/IT	114,000	122,000	127,000	130,000	163,000	169,000

Total Compensation by Function and Number of Employees

Function	Up to 100	100 to 1,000	250 to 5,000	1,000 10,000	5,000 to 10,000	Over
Managing Director	210,000	251,000	255,000	271,000	313,000	418,000
Personnel	102,000	104,000	133,000	151,000	170,000	214,000
Finance	119,000	116,000	135,000	153,000	165,000	255,000
Sales & Marketing	121,000	143,000	156,000	194,000	178,000	197,000
Manufacturing	117,000	122,000	150,000	165,000	191,000	221,000
Research & Development	(113,000)	136,000	147,000	159,000	170,000	191,000
EDP/IT	117,000	129,000	133,000	140,000	169,000	179,000

The above information has been provided by Kienbaum Personalberatung GmbH, Gummersbach.

Kienbaum and Partner, established in 1945, is one of the leading independent European consultancy groups. A member of EI – The European Independents –, Kienbaum offers a worldwide network of information and experience through its subsidiaries and partners. Services offered by Kienbaum cover management consultancy, developing countries consultancy, and personnel consultancy.

For further information, contact Johannes Etten at (0 22 61) 70 32 08.

Franchising has become a widely accepted form of business in the Federal Republic of Germany. In 1990, about 260 franchisors with approximately 12,500 franchisees were operating, some 180 of them organized in the German Franchise Association (Deutscher Franchise-Verband), which does not include automobile dealers, gas stations and hotels. The total turnover of all franchise operations in Germany in 1990 was estimated at DM 13 billion, with the beverage industry accounting for a considerable share. The annual growth of at least 10% in the past few years has always exceeded the growth rate of the German economy in general. Franchising is beginning to thrive in the new *Länder* as well, with over 1,400 eastern German franchisees active as independent partners of western German franchisors. Interestingly, a number of well-established western German companies which prior to the fall of the Wall did not use franchising have begun to do so with their eastern German partners. German franchisees are generally satisfied with how their business has developed – 88% of the franchisees surveyed in 1988 said they would repeat their original decision and three out of five would consider extending their outlets.

The federal government has frequently expressed its favourable attitude towards franchising and does not differentiate between networks of German or foreign origin. The same attitude prevails at the Federal Cartel Office (Bundeskartellamt), the only federal authority which deals with franchising issues on a regular basis.

While there are no national or regional statutes or regulations that cover franchising, the courts have issued an increasing number of rulings, in some instances attempting to define what "franchising" is. The European Court of Justice pronounced its widely noticed Pronuptia Judgement in 1986, followed on 30 November 1988 by the EC Commission with its Block Exemption Regulation No. 4087/88, which entered into force on 1 February 1989. Though not all-encompassing, this regulation gives the following definitions that are binding on all EC countries:

- A "franchise" is a package of industrial or intellectual property rights relating to trademarks, trade names, shop signs, utility models, designs, copyrights, know-how or patents, to be exploited from the resale of goods or the provision of services to end users.

- A "franchise agreement" is an agreement whereby one undertaking, the franchisor, grants the other, the franchisee, in exchange for direct or indirect financial consideration, the right to exploit a franchise for the purposes of marketing specified types of goods and/or services. At the very least, a franchise agreement includes obligations relating to the use of a common name or shop sign and a uniform presentation of contract premises. Other standard elements are the communication of know-how and ongoing provision of commercial or technical assistance from the franchisor to the franchisee.

- In a "master franchise agreement", one undertaking, the franchisor, grants the other, the master franchisee, the right to exploit a franchise for the purposes of concluding franchise agreements with third parties, the franchisees.

If one wants to establish a "franchise" network in Germany (or elsewhere in the EC), one has to fulfil these basic conditions and a few more. Otherwise, a distribution or cooperative relationship might be established but not a franchise arrangement.

A franchise business can be established in Germany in much the same way as in other countries. The most appropriate method for a foreign franchisor is either via a subsidiary, perhaps structured as a joint venture, or via a master franchise agreement. Direct cross-border franchising should be limited to specific or large-scale cases.

No foreign entrepreneur should think he can easily boost profits by selling the "map" of Germany and leaving the rest to the "master franchisee". When thinking of setting up a franchised business in Germany and before starting to look for a potential partner, any serious entrepreneur should first file an application for trademark registration (which is not expensive, but may take some time). Another key step is to conduct thorough research to determine whether the products or services will find a market (many service industries fall under the Handicrafts Code which gives stringent access rules) and if there is a supply of qualified labour for the business in question.

The most efficient way of setting up a business is then to establish a wholly owned subsidiary in the form of a GmbH (limited liability company) which requires minimum capital of DM 50,000 and a couple of months for registration. The subsidiary, which can be run either by a manager with solid experience at the parent company or by a locally recruited person who has been thoroughly trained at the franchisor's home base, should then establish the necessary one or two pilot outlets. Finding suitable and sufficient staff may not be easy, but there will be no need for complicated agreements since the franchisor owns the subsidiary. The pilot outlets should be used to adapt the system and the manuals to local standards. Once the system is functioning smoothly, it can be enlarged into a real franchise system with a master franchise agreement between franchisor and subsidiary, which then starts looking for franchisees, granting them unit franchise agreements under German laws. The subsidiary can also be transformed into a joint venture with a German partner. Experience shows that foreign systems transplanted via a subsidiary tend to be more stable and successful.

Another way of expanding a network into Germany is by setting up a master franchise. But it is an illusion to think that the master franchise can pay a substantial upfront fee and then bear all the development risks. If a foreign franchisor does not want to quickly ruin the name of its system in Germany, it has to decide whether it might be wise to start up with only a regional operation. Since errors are rarely reversible, it is vitally important to find the right person and provide him with thorough training – especially in his function as franchisor. The foreign franchisor must also take care to adapt (or participate in adapting) the system and manual to the German market and be involved in running the pilot operations.

Any master franchise agreement must take account of the following factors:

- Set initial and ongoing fees as a function of the real value of trademark, know-how and ongoing services of franchisor.
- Establish a reasonable development schedule.
- If the development schedule is not met, the choice must be made between terminating the agreement and assigning all franchises and other outlets to the franchisor and or forfeiting exclusivity for the existing network.

The master franchise agreement must also ensure that the master franchisee maintains control of all other franchisees while carefully specifying the consequences should the master franchisee and/or franchisees default. It must stipulate the consequences should the master agreement be terminated (whether on or ahead of schedule); the options are termination, continuance and/or assigning unit franchise agreements. In addition, the master agreement should include a model franchise agreement (adapted to German standards) and specify the applicable law and jurisdiction. The first choice should be the country where the master franchisee is based.

Whatever the case, a franchise requires – at least in the initial stages – substantial personal involvement and financial investment on the part of the franchisor. This is all the more true of franchisors seeking to make a direct start in eastern Germany, where franchising was a tremendous success in 1990. Forty to 50 networks with several thousand franchises are operating there – despite the negative general development of the eastern economy. Ignoring the day-to-day problems of doing business, eastern Germany still offers considerable advantages over other parts of Germany or Europe for a number of reasons. Not only is there a tremendous need for proven business formats replete with integrated know-how packages, but eastern Germany also has a large pool of highly qualified workers, especially in technical vocations and the skilled trades. For the moment, penetrating the eastern German market is easier as retail outlet density is only one-third that of the west. Franchisors can tap a wide range of substantial public investment incentives for new businesses, and many eastern Germans have a surprisingly good liquidity position. What is more, prime locations usually unavailable elsewhere are still to be had in eastern Germany, although they tend to be expensive.

Despite the current tendency of the media to highlight the economic difficulties facing eastern Germany, it is the view of this author that franchising opportunities merit close investigation.

Further general information can be obtained from:

Deutscher Franchise-Verband (DFV), (German Franchising Association)

St.-Paul-Str. 9, W-8000 München 2

Tel: (089) 53 50 27, Fax: (089) 53 13 231

The above information was provided by Albrecht Schulz, a specialist in franchising at Sigle, Loose, Schmidt-Diemitz & Partner (Stuttgart), and Vice-Chairman of Committee X International Franchising of the International Bar Association (IBA). For more information, contact Albrecht Schulz at (0711) 76 94 446.

Education and Training in Germany

The School System

The vast majority of German schools are run by the state, and private schools are few and far between. Each *Land* (including the five new ones) is responsible for its own school system. Thanks to this decentralization, school regulations and curricula differ (often widely) from *Land* to *Land*, although the *Länder* have concluded agreements to ensure that the overall structure is basically the same throughout the country (it is nevertheless true that neither pupils nor teachers can easily transfer from one *Land* school system to another). Attendance at all public schools and universities is free.

Almost all German teachers are civil servants on the *Länder* payrolls. All are required to have a university teaching degree and are paid on a uniform salary scale in force throughout Germany.

The German school system has the following salient features:

German children normally start school after their sixth birthday and are required to stay there until turning 18. Full-time attendance is mandatory for nine years, and for ten in some states, and the less academically minded can opt for part-time vocational schools thereafter.

The four years of *Grundschule* (primary or elementary school) end with a moment of truth when parents and/or teachers decide which of the three secondary school types is right for little Helmut or Birgit. The best performers go to a *Gymnasium*, an academically oriented high school leading to the university matriculation examination, the *Abitur*. Next comes *Realschule*, a kind of middle school leading to technical job training as well as medium-level managerial employment and civil service. It is possible (but difficult) to move from *Realschule* to institutions of higher education. At the lowest level is *Hauptschule* (general school).

The different school types are sometimes bundled together in a *Gesamt-schule* (comprehensive school). *Realschule* and *Hauptschule* graduates can go on to specialized vocational schools, technical schools and the like (as the diagram shows).

Pre-school education is voluntary but the demand for kindergartens far exceeds the supply. In socialist East Germany, there was room for each and every child in the kindergartens – a right that does not exist in post-unification Germany.

The East German school system, similar to the western system yet not without its idiosyncrasies, has since been scrapped, for better or worse. One interesting feature was a well-developed network of correspondence courses. Approximately 20% of university graduates got their degree while working on the side.

Vocational Training

There are only a handful of jobs-for-the-untrained in Germany; vocational training is the rule. It combines on-the-job training in a company authorized to train apprentices with instruction in a vocational school. This system is known as the dual system of vocational training.

There are about 400 recognized occupations or trades open to apprentices, more than 100 in the various crafts alone, and trainees may be future bakers, carpenters, plumbers, electricians, violin makers, opticians or, increasingly, office information electronics experts (to name but seven possibilities). Federal legislation sets the standards to be met by companies training apprentices and especially by instructors, who must not only be experts in their respective fields but must also know how to communicate these skills to the young. In general, it is the companies which finance on-the-job training, while the *Länder* pick up the bill for classroom instruction. (On the negative side: it does happen that some companies use their apprentices as poorly paid labour and neglect the training side of things.)

All students who have finished *Hauptschule* or *Realschule* or dropped out of *Gymnasium* must attend a vocational or trade school up to the age of 18. Approximately 60% of the classroom hours are devoted to specialized vocational instruction and 40% to general education.

Classroom teaching usually takes up one or two school days a week or three to four weeks of school learning alternating with practical hands-on training in the company. Part-time vocational schools generally concentrate on a select field, be it industry, commerce, agriculture or a mix of trades.

The two divided German states both practised this two-track system of vocational training. While an apprenticeship is usually a three-year undertaking in the west (and also in unified Germany), the old East German regime felt two years were enough before releasing its trainees into the working world. Since vocational training is governed by both federal law (the practical component) and

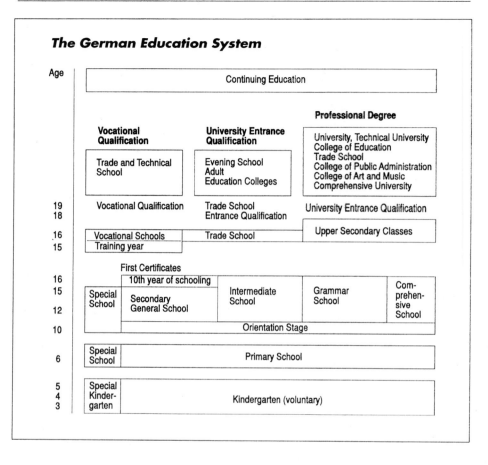

The German Education System

Age				

state regulations (the schooling component), two different agencies are now responsible for the adjustment in the east. West German vocational training legislation has been extended to the new *Länder* and covers the practical part of vocational training, including rights and duties of apprentices and companies, subject matter, compensation and so on. The old word for apprentice, *Lehrling,* has been officially replaced by *Auszubildender* (trainee).

Attendance at specialized vocational schools *(Berufsfachschulen)* can shorten or replace a trade apprenticeship. Young Germans conclude their vocational training by taking a theoretical and practical examination before an examining board of the respective *Kammer* (chamber), with successful candidates receiving a certificate of *Geselle* (journeyman's letter) or *Gehilfe* (assistant's letter).

For a number of years, apprenticeships have outnumbered would-be apprentices in western Germany – 540,000 applicants had 590,000 positions to choose from in the first quarter of 1991. The opposite situation prevails in the eastern *Länder*, with only 53,000 openings for 120,000 apprenticeship-seekers in March 1991. The federal government is subsidizing small eastern companies which take on apprentices in 1991. Apprenticeship subsidies are part of the DM 6.5 billion aid package with which the Federal Labour Office is financing professional training, retraining, job-creation and employment schemes in the new *Länder*.

The Institut der deutschen Wirtschaft reports that the German vocational training system has clearly reduced youth unemployment. While in western Germany only 4.2% of those under 25 were out of work in October 1990, the average for the EC was 16%.

Management Training and Continuing Education

Discussions in recent years about the pros and cons of MBAs are not unknown in Germany, although MBA programmes exist in only a few private elite institutions. The vast majority of business students attend regular state universities and major in economics and business administration, now horrendously overpopulated fields. Private business schools can, of course, restrict class sizes by charging stiff fees and setting high admission standards. These schools include the European Business School (Oestrich-Winkel), the Wirtschaftshochschule für Unternehmens-führung (Koblenz), the Universität Witten/Herdecke and the Europäische Wirts-chaftshochschule (Berlin).

Many companies attach great importance to the advanced training of their employees. Deutsche Bank provides no fewer than ten years of in-house specia-lized training for its most promising entry-level staff. Several other banks have followed suit. Other big companies, especially in the chemical industry and data processing, have set up their own advanced training programmes which groom the best and the brightest for top management slots.

In general, Germans in middle and upper management remain longer at a given company than their counterparts in other countries. According to a survey by Kienbaum Management Consultants, the average age of a managing director is 50; he entered his company at age 35 and became managing director five years later. The larger the company, the longer the climb up the corporate ladder: while the average age of executives in companies with fewer than 100 employees is 42, executives at companies with over 5,000 employees are ten years older.

Corporate Germany spent DM 26 billion on advanced training in 1987, according to a 1990 survey by the Institut der Deutschen Wirtschaft. This was three times more than in 1980 and a tenfold increase over 1972. German employees are legally entitled to advanced training for a specified number of days during their regular working hours.

Other kinds of continuing education are offered through *Abendgymnasien* (general secondary school evening classes which lead to university entrance qualifications), *Kollegs* (full-time institutes preparing adults for higher education) and *Volkshochschulen* (public institutions of adult education). *Volkshochschule* course offerings range from cooking, art appreciation and aerobics to foreign languages, data processing and business skills. The schools are supported by cities and communities as well as through financial assistance from the state and can be found in any major community.

Ilka Eßmüller

Who's What in German Companies

German	British	American
Aktiengesellschaft (AG)	*Public Limited Company (Plc)*	*Stock Corporation*
Vorsitzender des Vorstandes	Managing Director	President and Chief Executive Officer
or Sprecher des Vorstandes	Chief Executive Officer Chairman of the Board of Management	Chief Executive Officer President Chairman of the Executive Board Chairman of the Board of Management
Mitglied des Vorstandes	Member of the Board of Management	Member of the Executive Board Member of the Board of Management Executive Vice President
Vorsitzender des Aufsichtsrates	Chairman of the Supervisory Board	Chairman of the Supervisory Board
Mitglied des Aufsichtsrates	Member of the Supervisory Board	Member of the Supervisory Board
Generalbevollmächtigter	General Manager	General Manager
Arbeitsdirektor	Director of Labour Relations	Executive for Labor Relations
Prokurist	Authorised Officer	Authorized Officer
Handlungsbevollmächtigter	Assistant Manager	Assistant Manager
Vorsitzender des Verwaltungsrates	Chairman of the Administrative Board	Chairman of the Administrative Board
Beirat	Advisory Board	Advisory Board
Hauptversammlung	Shareholders' Meeting General Meeting	Stockholders Meeting Shareholders Meeting
GmbH	*Private Limited Company*	*Closed Corporation Privately Held Corporation*
Geschäftsführer	Director	General Manager Managing Director
Vorsitzender der Geschäftsführung	Managing Director Chairman of the Board of Directors	Chief Executive Officer President Chairman of the Board of Management
Gesellschafterversammlung	Shareholders' Meeting General Meeting	Stockholders Meeting
Gesellschafter	Shareholder/Member	Shareholder/Stockholder

German	British	American
OHG	*Partnership*	*Partnership*
Gesellschafter	Partner	Partner
Geschäftsführender Partner	Managing Partner	Managing Partner
Kommanditgesellschaft	*Limited Partnership*	*Limited Partnership*
Komplementär	General Partner	General Partner
Persönlich haftender		
Gesellschafter	General Partner	General Partner
Kommanditist	Limited Partner	Limited Partner
Geschäftsführender		
Gesellschafter	Managing Partner	Managing Partner
GmbH & Co. KG	*Limited Partnership with*	*Limited Partnership with*
	Limited Company	*Limited Company*
	as General Partner	*as General Partner*
Einzelkaufmann	*Sole Proprietor/Sole Trader*	*Sole Proprietor*
Geschäftsinhaber	Proprietor	Proprietor
Geschäftsteilhaber	Co-owner/Co-Proprietor	Co-owner
Alleininhaber	Sole Proprietor	Sole Proprietor
Verband	*Association*	*Association*
Geschäftsführer	Director	Managing Director
Hauptgeschäftsführer	Managing Director	General Executive Manager
Präsident	President	President
Vorstand/Präsidium	Board of Directors	Board of Directors
	Executive Board	Executive Board
Vorsitzender	Chairman of the Executive	Chairman of the Board
	Board	of Directors
	Chairman of the Board	
	of Directors	
Ehrenvorsitzender	Honorary Chairman of	Honorary Chairman of
	the Board of Directors	the Board of Directors
Hauptausschuß	Executive Committee	Executive Committee
Sonstige Titel	*Other titles*	*Other titles*
Präsident	President	President
Ehrenpräsident	Honorary President	Honorary President
Generaldirektor	General Manager	General Manager
Stellvertretender		
Generaldirektor	Assistant General Manager	Assistant General Manager

German	British	American
Generalbevollmächtigter	General Manager	General Manager
Direktor	Manager	Manager
Abteilungsdirektor	Division Manager	Division Manager
Prokurist	Authorised Officer	Authorized Officer
Handlungsbevollmächtigter	Assistant Manager	Assistant Manager
Bevollmächtigter	Authorised Representative	Authorized Representative
Leiter der Rechtsabteilung	Head of Legal Department	Head of Legal Department
		General Counsel
Leiter der Personalabteilung	Head of Personnel Department	Head of Personnel Department
	Personnel Manager	Personnel Manager
Betriebsdirektor	Production Manager	Production Manager
Werksleiter	Works Manager	Plant Manager
Hauptabteilungsleiter	Head of Division	Head of Division
Bereichsleiter	Head of Department	Head of Department
Betriebsleiter	Production Manager	Production Manager

Source: *Handelsblatt*

Major Trade Fairs

Germany is the world market leader in the trade fair industry – more than 100 of the 400 major international trade fairs take place in the Federal Republic. The past ten years have been a period of impressive growth for the German trade fair industry; since the early Eighties, the number of German exhibitors has risen by 51%, while 83% more foreign companies have chosen to display their wares at German fairs. Trade fair agencies across the country have met this increasing demand by expanding their exhibition hall capacity by 43%. No slowdown is in sight; in 1989 the magic number of 100,000 exhibitors was finally surpassed – representing an increase of 9.5% over 1988. More than five million sq metres of exhibition space was rented out (+12%), and the number of visitors rose 27.1% to 9.8 million. While the figures for 1990 are not yet available, it appears that the year was just as successful as 1989, with 1991 expected to continue this trend.

The above figures represent an average; Hanover's Deutsche Messe AG was able to post even more impressive results and consolidate its position as the world's largest trade fair company. Total turnover of the Deutsche Messe AG rose 48% in 1989 to DM 317 million.

The trade fair branch has now become a significant service industry in Germany and accounts for DM 11 billion in total turnover. Part of the reason for this strength is the decentralized structure of the trade fair industry. Unlike other European countries which have one or two major venues (such as Milan, Paris, Birmingham and London, Madrid and Barcelona, Brussels or Luxembourg), Germany boasts five major trade fair cities: Hanover, Frankfurt, Munich, Düsseldorf and Cologne.

Hanover is Germany's top trade fair venue, with 724,000 sq metres of indoor and outdoor exhibition space. But when measured in terms of the number of visitors, centrally located Frankfurt took the lead in 1989 with 2.6 million visitors as compared to Hanover's 2.3 million.

In East Germany, Leipzig was traditionally considered to be the major trade fair city for all of Eastern Europe. Under the socialist regime, Leipzig's spring and autumn capital goods trade fairs attracted a total of 800,000 visitors and 10,000 exhibitors from all over Eastern Europe. But Leipzig now finds itself unable to compete with the established western German trade fairs and in desperate need of a new concept. Indeed, many exhibitors at the Autumn Fair in 1990 expressed disappointment at the poor infrastructure, lack of service and scarcity of Eastern European exhibitors or visitors. Leipzig is now attempting to transform itself into a more regional and specialized exhibition venue, but it faces tough competition from the established sites in western Germany.

Many western German trade fair agencies are embarking on major program-mes to improve or expand their exhibition space. The association which represents Germany's major trade fair agencies, AUMA, estimated that in 1989 more than DM 306 million was invested to expand or renovate exhibition space and that by 1993 more than DM 900 million will have been invested. Düsseldorf, for example, has embarked on a DM 66 million project to smarten up its fair grounds. By 1992, Cologne will have built DM 200 million in new exhibition halls. But Frankfurt's plans are the most ambitious: by 1994, more than DM 800 million will have been spent on improving or expanding its exhibition site.

Munich too has plans to extend its capacity – partly because it has also dramatically increased the number of exhibitions and is bursting at the seams. But it will not be able to expand significantly until 1997, when the trade fair will take over the old airport site at Riem.

Berlin, which as West Berlin was not considered one of the major venues in Germany, now finds itself in an extremely good position. Although Berlin has for some time hosted two major fairs, the Green Week garden show and the International Tourism Exchange, it remained relatively unimportant as a trade fair centre because of its isolated location, its lack of sufficient top quality hotels and its short supply of exhibition space (86,200 sq metres). Now that a private investor has proposed investing DM 1.2 billion to double Berlin's exhibition capacity, the latter problem may be solved. As a sign of things to come, the Association for the German Automotive Industry announced last year that it will stage the commercial vehicles section of the International Automotive Exhibition in Berlin in 1992. The show has simply grown too large for Frankfurt, which will continue to host the larger passenger vehicle exhibition.

It was a major coup for Berlin to convince the commercial vehicle exhibition to move away from Frankfurt, and it underscores a growing competitiveness between the various venues. So for example, the first ever "Cologne Hi-Fi" was staged in 1990 – strategically scheduled for the off-year of Berlin's major biennial TV and radio trade fair. But Berlin has now struck back, and this year plans to host the SHK trade fair for heating and air-conditioning technology in the off-year of the biennial ISH (sanitation, heating and air-conditioning) trade fair in Frankfurt.

Germany is seeking to increase its competitiveness overseas by exporting trade fairs to foreign countries. The Frankfurt trade fair agency, for example, has organized its popular Interstoff textile trade fair in Hong Kong, while the Cologne trade fair is staging the CIA '91 (a specialized chemicals and equipment exhibition) in Singapore, and the Munich agency has arranged SIB '91 (an import-export trade fair) in the Soviet Union.

The Düsseldorf trade fair agency has adopted a different international strategy. It has set up a joint venture agreement with McCormick Place in Chicago to cooperate in the areas of training and marketing, and even to hold joint exhibitions. This arrangement makes sense, since both organizations have similar trade fairs: Düsseldorf's printing trade fair Drupa is equivalent to Chicago's Print; Düsseldorf's "K" is similar to Chicago's National Plastics Exhibition, and Interpack in Düsseldorf is equal to Chicago's PackExpo.

David Hart

We have retained the German spelling of the city names; for the uninitiated, they translate as follows:

Hannover	Hanover
Köln	Cologne
München	Munich
Nürnberg	Nuremberg

1991

Date	Location	Fair

October

Date	Location	Fair
Oct. 6-10	Dresden	Restaurant Supplies Exhibition
Oct. 8-11	Düsseldorf	Industrial Safety + Occupational Health
Oct. 9-14	Frankfurt	Frankfurt Book Fair
Oct. 16-18	Bad Dürkheim	"EFA'91" Electronic Trade Fair
Oct. 16-20	Dresden	Modernization + Restoration of Old Buildings
Oct. 17-19	Essen	International Trade Fair for Refrigeration and Air Conditioning
Oct. 19-27	Hamburg	International Boat Show Hamburg with EMTEC Trade Days
Oct. 21-26	München	Computers and Communications – International Trade Fair and International Congress
Oct. 22-24	Frankfurt	International Trade Fair for Clothing Textiles
Oct. 22-24	Hannover	International Trade Fair + Congress for Biotechnology
Oct. 23-26	Frankfurt	MANAGEMENT & MARKETING SERVICES – International Market for Marketing and Communication
Oct. 23-27	Düsseldorf	REHA – Rehabilitation Assistance for Handicapped People

Date	Location	Fair

November

Nov. 1-6	Leipzig	Construction + Building Trade Fair
Nov. 5-7	Pirmasens	Pirmasens International Leather Exhibition
Nov. 6-11	Köln	International Trade Fair for Leisure, Sports and Pool Facilities
Nov. 8-10	Dresden	Trade Fair for Carpentry, Woodworking and Plastics Processing
Nov. 12-16	München	International Trade Fair for Electronics Production
Nov.12-Dec.1	Magdeburg	Regional Christmas Exhibition
Nov. 14-16	Nürnberg	European Trade Fair for the Brewery and Beverage Industries
Nov. 16-25	Halle	Regional Consumer Goods Exhibition
Nov. 20-23	Düsseldorf	Diagnostica – Therapeutica – Technica – Informatica – Biotechnica – Juristica, International Congress and Trade Fair
Nov. 21-26	Leipzig	Trade and Gastronomy Trade Fair

December

Dec. 5-10	Leipzig	Tourist and Camping Trade Fair
Dec. 6-12	Halle	Regional Christmas Exhibition

1992

January

Jan. 6-9	Hannover	World Trade Fair for Carpets and Floor Coverings
Jan. 8-11	Frankfurt	International Trade Fair for Home and Household Textiles
Jan. 14-15	Köln	It's Cologne – International Trend Show for Fashion Cologne
Jan. 17-26	Berlin	International Green Week Berlin
Jan. 18-26	Düsseldorf	boot Düsseldorf – International Boat Show
Jan. 21-26	Köln	International Furniture Fair
Jan. 22-25	Frankfurt	International Amusement and Vending Trade Fair
Jan. 22-29	Essen	Building in Europe/Building Trade Fair with Congresses
Jan. 23-26	Offenbach	International Leather Goods Fair
Jan. 25-29	Frankfurt	International Trade Fair for Consumer Goods

Date	Location	Fair

February

Feb. 2-4	Düsseldorf	CPD – Collections Premieren Düsseldorf
Feb. 2-6	Köln	International Sweets and Biscuits Fair
Feb. 6-12	Nürnberg	International Toy Fair with a Special Show of Model Construction Kits and Hobby Crafts
Feb. 7-9	Köln	International Menswear Fair Cologne/International Casualwear and Young Fashion Fair Cologne
Feb. 7-10	München	International Trade Fair for Watches, Clocks, Jewellery, Precious Stones, Silverware and Their Manufacturing Equipment
Feb. 14-16	Essen	International Trade Fair for Plants, Horticultural Equipment, Florist' Requisites
Feb. 15-19	Frankfurt	International Trade Fair for Consumer Goods
Feb. 16-18	München	International Fashion Fair
Feb. 17-21	Dortmund	European Education Fair
Feb. 18-21	Köln	International Fair for Home Appliances, Household Technology, Kitchens and Kitchenware
Feb. 19-25	Düsseldorf	International Fair and Congress Pre-Press and Communication
Feb. 22-27	Stuttgart	International Trade Fair for the Hotel, Catering and Confectionery Trades
Feb. 23-26	Wiesbaden	International Trade Fair for Confectionery, Cafe, Confiserie, Ice Cream
Feb.27-Mar.1	München	International Trade Fair for Sports Equipment and Fashion
February/March	Köln	International Baby to Teenager Fair Cologne

March

March	Frankfurt	International Trade Fair for Musical Instruments and Accessories
Mar. 7-12	Berlin	International Tourism Exchange ITB Berlin
Mar. 8-13	Düsseldorf	International Fashion Trade Fair with Trade Fair for Lingerie, Foundations, Swimwear
Mar. 8-11	Köln	International Hardware Fair – Tools, Locks + Fittings, Building and DIY Supplies
Mar. 10-14	Stuttgart	International Trade Fair for Heating and Air Conditioning

Date	Location	Fair
Mar. 11-18	Hannover	World Centre for Office, Information and Telecommunications Technology
Mar. 13-16	Nürnberg	International Trade Fair for Hunting and Sporting Arms and Accessories
Mar. 13-18	Hamburg	International Exhibition for the Hotel, Restaurant, Catering, Bakery and Confectionery Trades
Mar. 14-18	Leipzig	Leipzig Fair – Trade Fair for Consumer Goods
Mar. 14-20	Leipzig	Leipzig Fair – Technical Fair
Mar. 14-22	München	International Light Industries and Handicrafts Fair – The Fair for Small and Medium-Sized Enterprises
Mar. 20-23	Düsseldorf	International Shoe Fair

April

Date	Location	Fair
Apr. 1-8	Hannover	HANNOVER FAIR Industry
Apr. 6-10	Düsseldorf	International Wire and Cable Trade Fair
Apr. 6-10	Düsseldorf	International Tube and Pipe Trade Fair
Apr. 6-11	Köln	International Dental Show
Apr. 4-14	München	International Trade Fair for Construction Equipment and Building Material Machines
Apr. 7-9	Frankfurt	International Trade Fair for Clothing Textiles
Apr. 9-12	Frankfurt	FUR & FASHION Frankfurt
Apr. 10-12	Karlsruhe	Trade Exhibition of Horticulture South
Apr. 25-May 3	Saarbrücken	International Saar Fair
Apr. 28-30	Frankfurt	International Trade Fair for Public Design

May

Date	Location	Fair
May	Frankfurt	International Trade Fair for Information Management
May	Köln	International Fair for Food Manufacturing and Processing
May	Pirmasens	Pirmasens International Leather Exhibition
May 1-4	Köln	International Trade Fair for Opthalmic Optics in Association with the Annual Congress of WVAO
May 5-8	München	International Trade Fair for Biochemical and Instrumental Analysis with International Conference
May 5-8	Stuttgart	Computer Aided Technologies – International Exhibition and User Congress

Date	Location	Fair
May 5-9	Düsseldorf	Exhibition of Manufacturing Technology and Automation
May 5-10	Nürnberg	International Trade Fair for Pet Supplies
May 9-17	Berlin	International Bakery Exhibition
May 9-17	Hannover	International Motor Show Commercial Vehicles
May 16-21	Frankfurt	International Trade Fair for the Meat Industry
May 19-22	Nürnberg	International Trade Exhibition of Medical and Hospital Equipment and Supplies
May 25-29	Düsseldorf	Technology for Environmental Protection – International Trade Fair and Congress
May 27-30	Essen	International Trade Fair for Tyres and Tyre Technology
May 27-30	Hannover	Specialized Trade Fair for Roof, Wall and Insulation Technology
May 27-Jun. 1	Stuttgart	International Trade Exhibition for Viticulture and Enology, Cultivation and Processing of Fruit, Bottling and Packaging Technology

June

June 6-10	Berlin	Import Fair Berlin "Partners for Progess"
June 23-27	Nürnberg	International Trade Fair for Metalworking

July

July 14-15	Köln	It's Cologne – International Trend Show for Fashion Cologne

August

Aug. 2-4	Düsseldorf	CPD – Collections Premieren Düsseldorf
Aug. 14-16	Köln	International Menswear Fair Cologne/International Casualwear and Young Fashion Fair Cologne
Aug. 16-18	München	International Fashion Fair
Aug. 22-25	Offenbach	International Leather Goods Fair
Aug. 22-26	Frankfurt	International Trade Fair for Consumer Goods
Aug. 18-30	Karlsruhe	Congress and Exhibition of Pharmaceutical Products, Medical Equipment, Technical Products
Aug.30-Sept.1	Köln	GAFA – International Garden Trade Fair

Date	Location	Fair
Aug.30-Sept.1	Köln	SPOGA – International Trade Fair of Sports Goods, Camping Equipment and Garden Furniture

September

September	Köln	International Baby to Teenager Fair Cologne
Sept. 1-4	München	International Trade Fair for Sports Equipment and Fashion
Sept. 1-5	Stuttgart	International Exhibition of Metalworking
Sept. 5-9	Leipzig	Leipzig Fair – Trade Fair for Consumer Goods
Sept. 5-11	Leipzig	Leipzig Fair – Technical Fair
Sept. 6-9	Düsseldorf	International Fashion Trade Fair with Trade Fair for Lingerie, Foundations, Swimwear
Sept. 9-13	Frankfurt	International Trade Fair for Motor Car Workshop and Service Station Equipment, Spare Parts and Accessories
Sept. 10-13	Nürnberg	European Trade Fair for Gardening, Landscaping and Sportsground Construction
Sept. 15-17	Hannover	Biotechnica – International Trade Fair + Congress for Biotechnology
Sept. 16-22	Köln	World's Fair of Imaging Systems – Photo – Cine – Video/photofinishing Professional Media
Sept. 18-21	Düsseldorf	International Shoe Fair
Sept. 19-27	Friedrichshafen	International Water Sports Exhibition
Sept. 22-26	Düsseldorf	International Trade Fair – Machinery – Equipment – Applications – Products
Sept. 26-28	München	International Trade Fair for Watches, Clocks, Jewellery, Precious Stones, Silverware and Their Manufacturing Equipment
Sept.26-Oct.4	Essen	International Caravan Exhibition
Sept.29-Oct.3	Hamburg	International Shipping and Marine Technology Market with Congress
Sept.30-Oct.3	Stuttgart	International Exhibition and Conference for Telecommunications
Sept.30-Oct.4	Köln	International Bicycle and Motor Cycle Exhibition
Sept.30-Oct.5	Frankfurt	Frankfurt Book Fair

Date	Location	Fair

October

Oct. 5-10	Düsseldorf	Market for Innovations in Measurement and Automation
Oct. 7-10	Stuttgart	International Trade Fair with Congress
Oct. 8-10	Nürnberg	IKK – International Trade Fair for Refrigerating and Air Conditioning
Oct. 10-14	Stuttgart	International Trade Fair for Swimming Pools, Medicinal Baths, Saunas and Equipment for Baths
Oct. 10-18	Berlin	Motor Show Berlin
Oct. 19-23	München	International Trade Fair for Computer Integration in Industry and International Congress
Oct. 22-27	Köln	International Office Trade Fair
Oct.29-Nov.5	Düsseldorf	International Trade Fair Plastics + Rubber
Oct. 29-31	Frankfurt	International Trade Fair for Clothing Textiles
Oct.31-Nov.8	Hamburg	International Boat Show Hamburg with EMTEC Trade Days

November

November	Düsseldorf	International Trade Fair Hotels, Gastronomy, Catering
November	Düsseldorf	International Light and Sound Entertainment Fair
November	Nürnberg	European Trade Fair for the Brewery and Beverage Industries
November	Pirmasens	Pirmasens International Leather Exhibition
Nov. 1-7	Essen	International Sheet Metal Working Exhibition
Nov. 3-7	Frankfurt	8th International Exhibition of Dairy Technology and Food Processing
Nov. 10-14	München	International Trade Fair for Components and Assemblies in Electronics
Nov. 18-21	Düsseldorf	Diagnostica – Therapeutica – Technica – Informatica – Biotechnica – Juristica, International Congress and Trade Fair
Nov. 24-27	Essen	International Security Exhibition with Congress

Advertising

Press

The German public has a wide choice of daily, weekly and monthly newspapers and magazines – around 2,600 in all, excluding trade and specialized journals. Detailed information on these and other advertising media can be found in *Leitfaden durch Presse und Werbung*, published annually by:
Stamm-Verlag GmbH
Goldammerweg 16
W-4300 Essen 1

Circulation figures of German newspapers are relatively low (compared to the UK, for example), partly because there are so many of them (around 375 daily newspapers in western Germany alone) and partly because most dailies have regional rather than nationwide sales. The best known nationally circulating dailies are:

Bild Zeitung (Hamburg)	(5,346,800)
Die Welt (Hamburg)	(304,100)
Frankfurter Allgemeine Zeitung (F.A.Z.) (Frankfurt)	(433,000)
Süddeutsche Zeitung (SZ) (Munich)	(421,700)
Handelsblatt (Düsseldorf) (five times a week)	(142,300)
Frankfurter Rundschau (Frankfurt)	(217,700)
Sächsische Zeitung (Dresden)	(525,000)
Berliner Zeitung (Berlin)	(303,517)

Of the numerous major daily newspapers in eastern Germany, many have been placed in receivership since unification and are gradually being reorganized through management buyouts and takeovers by western publishing groups.

Many German chambers of commerce publish monthly journals which can be a useful means of bringing products to the attention of businessmen in particular areas.

Trade unions publish their own journals, some of which are widely used by advertisers, particularly those selling consumer goods. One such newspaper is the weekly trade union newspaper *Welt der Arbeit*.

Cinema

Moviegoers in over 3,000 cinemas can watch up to a half hour of trailers while settling in to their seats. Cinema adverts are produced and placed by specialized firms throughout the country. A list of producers and distributors of advertising films is given in the *Leitfaden* report on advertising in Germany mentioned above. Prices for the showing of publicity films vary, depending on the size of the cinema.

Display

There are good opportunities for display advertising in towns and villages throughout Germany. There are billboards as well as advertising display space in or on public conveyances. An advertising agent should be consulted for this medium.

Mail

The delivery of advertising circulars through the mail has become very popular in Germany in recent years. The Bundespost (federal post office) operates a system under which it is possible for publicity materials and small samples to be sent through the mail to all households and post office boxes. Details on direct mail promotion are available from Zentralauskunftsstelle für Postwurfsendungen (Postamt I, Zeil 10, W-6000 Frankfurt 2).

In addition, there are private companies which offer services similar to those of the post office and which supply address lists of target groups of businesses or professionals, from doctors and architects to wholesale dealers and cafés. Some will handle mailings if the materials are provided to them. Three such companies are:

Verlag Koop GmbH
Zimmerstr. 9-11, Postfach 8108, W-4000 Düsseldorf 1
Tel: (02 11) 34 40 34, Fax: (02 11) 33 05 37, Telex: 08 581 836

Schober OHG
Max-Eyth-Str. 6-10, Postfach 1000, W-7257 Ditzingen 5 Hirschlanden
Tel: (0 71 56) 304-1, Fax: (0 71 56) 304-369, Telex: 7 245 238

Merkur Direktwerbegesellschaft mbH & Co KG, Adressenverlag
Kapellenstr. 44, Postfach 206, W-3352 Einbeck
Tel: (0 55 61) 314-0, Fax: (0 55 61) 314-33, Telex: 965 624

These firms also sell names and addresses for companies' own use in direct advertising campaigns. Catalogues describing the range of services are available.

Radio and Television

The public broadcasting companies carry commercials which are grouped together at regularly scheduled air times. Western Germany has the following TV stations:
Norddeutscher Rundfunk (Hamburg)
Bayerischer Rundfunk (Munich)
Süddeutscher Rundfunk (Stuttgart)
Südwestfunk (Baden-Baden)
Hessischer Rundfunk (Frankfurt)
Radio Bremen (Bremen)
Sender Freies Berlin (Berlin)
Saarländischer Rundfunk (Saarbrücken)
Westdeutscher Rundfunk (Cologne)
Zweites Deutsches Fernsehen (ZDF) (Mainz)

The first German television network, Arbeitsgemeinschaft der öffentlich-rechtlichen Rundfunkanstalten Deutschlands (ARD), links together the first nine organizations listed above. The rate for a commercial on either of the two nationwide state-sponsored television networks, ZDF or ARD, depends on whether the broadcast is national or regional as well as on the time of day and season of the year. Television advertising on these state-sponsored networks is restricted to the period from 6 to 8 p.m. Radio advertising is broadcast in the mornings as well.

Pay television networks, chiefly SAT 1 and RTL Plus, target the German broadcast market and carry advertising at all times of the day. The stations are available to viewers with cable television feeds or satellite dishes. Several commercial radio broadcasters also beam advertising to the German market.

Useful Contacts

Since many of the addresses given below are useful for a variety of purposes, they could re-appear under a variety of headings. To avoid repetition, we give each one in full only once and thereafter indicate where it can be found.

The ultimate reference book for organizations in Germany is the OECKL. (Festland Verlag GmbH, Postfach 20 05 61, 5300 Bonn 2). This "bible" is in German; it does not contain a description of the organizations listed.

Federal and Länder Level

Bundesministerium für Wirtschaft (BMW)
Minstry of Economics
Villemombler Str. 76, W-5300 Bonn 1
Tel: (0228) 6 15-1; Fax: (0228) 615-44 36

Bundesamt für Wirtschaft
Federal Office of Economics
Frankfurter Str. 29-31, W-6236 Eschborn 1
Tel: (06196) 4 04-0; Fax: (06196) 4 04-2 12
The Bundesamt für Wirtschaft is an executive authority of federal economic administration under the jurisdiction of the Federal Ministry of Economics. Laws, directives, and other regulations and guidelines of the federal government and the EC are implemented here in the form of specific, individual decisions in the areas of foreign trade, promotion of industry, energy supply and, in part, environmental protection.

Bundesanstalt für Außenhandelsinformation
Federal Office of Foreign Trade Information
Agrippastr. 87-93, (P.O. Box 108007),
W-5000 Köln 1
Tel: (0221) 20 57-0; Fax: (0221) 20 57-2 12; -2 75

Wirtschaftsministerkonferenz der Länder
Conference of the Economics Ministers of the *Länder*
Görrestr. 15, Bundeshaus, W-5300 Bonn 1
Tel: (0228) 16-41 06, -41 68;
Fax: (0228) 16-77 75
Coordinating body of the Länder economics ministers; addresses of the respective Länder economics ministries can be obtained here.

Bundesministerium der Finanzen
Ministry of Finance
Graurheindorfer Str. 108, W-5300 Bonn
Tel: (0228) 6 82-0; Fax: (0228) 6 82-44 20; -44 66

Bundesministerium für Forschung und Technologie
Ministry for Research and Technology
Heinemannstr. 2, W-5300 Bonn-Bad Godesberg
Tel: (0228) 59-0; Fax: (0228) 59-36 01

Treuhandanstalt
(public trust authority)
Leipziger Str. 5 - 7, O-1086 Berlin
Tel: (030) 31 54-0; Fax: (030) 31 54-13 20

For Treuhand Bonn office and regional offices in the new *Länder*, see pages 118-119.

Bundesanstalt für Arbeit
Federal Employment Office
Regensburger Str. 104, W-8500 Nürnberg 30
Tel: (0911) 179-0; Fax: (0911) 17-21 23
*Umbrella organization for all employment
agencies (of Länder and municipalities),
which coordinates professional guidance/coun-
seling, job opportunities and openings, furthe-
ring of vocational and professional training,
retraining, provision of payments to create
jobs, processing of unemployment payments
and benefits.*

Chambers of Industry and Commerce (Germany)

Deutscher Industrie- und Handelstag (DIHT)
Federation of German Chambers of Industry
and Commerce
Adenauerallee 148, W-5300 Bonn 1
Tel: (0228) 1 04-0; Fax: (0228) 10 4-1 58
*Addresses of Chambers of Industry and Com-
merce in the various Länder and cities can be
obtained from the DIHT*

Vertretung des Deutschen Industrie- und
Handelstages bei der EG
EC Liaison Office of the Association of the
German Chambers of Industry and Commerce
49a, Boulevard Clovis, B-1040 Brussels
Tel: (32-2) 2 30-29 00; Fax: (32 2) 2 30-03 99

Deutsche Gruppe der Internationalen Handels-
kammer
(German section of the International Chamber
of Commerce)
Kolumbastr. 5, W-5000 Köln 1
Tel: (0221) 21 95 31-32; Fax: (0221) 23 03 33

Selected List of German Chambers of Commerce (Abroad)

Austria
German Chamber of Commerce in Austria
(Deutsche Handelskammer in Österreich)
Wiedner Hauptstr. 142, A-1050 Vienna
Tel: (43 1) 55 45 65; Fax: (43 1) 55 45 65 26

Australia
German-Australian Chamber of Industry and
Commerce
St. Andrews House, Level 2, 464 Kent Street
(P.O. Box A 980), Sydney, South N.S.W. 2000
Tel: (6 12) 2 61-44 75, -44 78; Fax: (6 12) 2 67-
38 07

Belgium-Luxembourg
German-Belgian-Luxembourgian Chamber of
Commerce
(Chambre de Commerce DEBELUX)
21 Avenue du Boulevard, Manhattan Center,
B-1210 Brussels
Tel: (32 2) 2 18-50 40; Fax: (32 2) 2 18-47 58

DEBLELUX Handelskammer
Cäcilienstr. 46, W-5000 Köln 1
Tel: (0221) 21 39 86, 21 75 00; Fax: (0221) 21 63
70

Canada
Canadian German Chamber of Industry and
Commerce Inc.
480 University Ave., Suite 1410, Toronto, Ont.
M5G 1V2
Tel: (1 416) 5 98-33 55; Fax: (1 416) 5 98-18 40

Denmark
Representative of the German Economy
Börsen, 1217 Copenhagen K
Tel: (45 33) 9 13-3 35; Fax: (45 33) 9 13-1 16

Egypt
German-Arab Chamber of Commerce
3 Abu El Feda Street, 14th Floor, Cairo-Zamalek
(P.O. Box 385, 11511 Ataba-Cairo)
Tel: (2 02) 3 41-36 62, 3 41-36 64;
Fax: (2 02) 3 41-36 63

Finland
German-Finnish Chamber of Commerce
Kalevankatu 3 B (P.O. Box 83), 00101 Helsinki
Tel: (35 80) 64 28 55; Fax: (35 80) 64 28 59

France
German-French Chamber of Industry and
Commerce (Chambre Franco-Allemande de
Commerce et d'Industrie)
18, rue Balard, 75015 Paris
Tel: (33 1) 40 58 35 35; Fax: (33 1) 45 75 47 39

Greece
German-Greek Chamber of Commerce and
Industry
Dorileou Str. 10-12/IV, 11521 Athens
Tel: (30 1) 6 44 45-02, -24, -46;
Fax: (30 1) 6 44 51 75

India
Indo-German Chamber of Commerce
Marker Towers "E", 1st floor, Cuffe Parade,
Bombay-400005
(P.O. Box 11092, Bombay-40020)
Tel: (91 22) 2 18-61 31, -61 18, -79 02, -79 03;
Fax: (91 22) 2 18- 05 23

Italy
German-Italian Chamber of Commerce
(Camera di Commercio Italo-Germanica)
Via Napo Torriani 29, 20124 Milan
Tel: (39 2) 66 98-83 51, -83 52, -83 53;
Fax: (39 2) 66 98-09 64

Japan
German Chamber of Commerce and Industry
in Japan
Akasaka Tokyo Building, Nagata-cho 2-14-3,
Chiyoda-ku/Tokyo 100
(Zainichi Doitsu Shoko Kaigisho, Central
P.O.Box 588, Tokyo 100-91)
Tel: (81 3) 35 81-98 81, -98 82, -98 83;
Fax: (81 3) 35 93-13 50

Netherlands
Deutsch-Niederländische Handelskammer
(Nederlands-Duitse Kamer van Koophandel)
Nassauplein 30, 2585 EC The Hague (Postbus
80533, 2508 GM The Hague)
Tel: (31-70) 3 61 42 51; Fax: (31-70) 3 63 22 18

Deutsch-Niederländische Handelskammer
Freiligrathstr. 25, W-4000 Düsseldorf
(P.O.Box 32 02 13)
Tel: (0211) 4 98 72 01; Fax: (0211) 4 92 04 15

Norway
German-Norwegian Chamber of Commerce
Drammenscien 40, 0255 Oslo 2
(P.O. Box 2853 Solly, 0230 Oslo 2)
Tel: (47 2) 44 70 79; Fax: (47 2) 83 08 88

Poland
Delegate of the German Economy
(Delegatura Gospodarki Niemieckicj w Polsce)
Ul. Miodowa 14, 00-246 Warsaw
(P.O. Box 439, 00-950 Warsaw)
Tel: (48 22) 6 35 33-53; -54; -55; -56;
Fax: (48 22) 6 35 81 06

Portugal
German-Portuguese Chamber of Industry and
Commerce
(Camara de Comérçio e Indústria Luso-Alema)
Av. da Liberdade, 38-20, 1200 Lisbon
Tel: (35 11) 3 47 27 24; Fax: (35 11) 34 67 12 50

Saudi-Arabia
German-Saudi Arabian Liaison Office for Eco-
nomic Affairs
Dhabah Street, 5th Floor, Suite 1, Chamber of
Commerce Building (P.O. Box 6 16 95), Riyadh
11575
Tel: (966 1) 4 03-15 00; Fax: (966 1) 4 03-51 21

South Korea
Korean-German Chamber of Commerce and
Industry
45, 4-Ka, Namdaemun-ro, Chung-Ku, KCCI
Bldg. 10th floor, (P.O. Box 4963), Seoul 100-649
(82 2) 7 76-15 46;-15 49; Fax: (82 2) 7 56-78 28

Spain
German Chamber of Commerce in Spain
Cámara de Comercio Alemana para España
Paseo de la Castellana, 18, E-28046 Madrid
Tel: (34 1) 5 75 40 00; Fax: (34 1) 4 35 02 16

Sweden
German-Swedish Chamber of Commerce
Tysk-Svenska Handelskammaren
Munkbron 9 (P.O. Box 1223),
S-11182 Stockholm
Tel: (46 8) 21 75-54; -61; -69;
Fax: (46 8) 7 90 30 98

Switzerland
Handelskammer Deutschland-Schweiz
Chamber of Commerce Germany-Switzerland
Talacker 41, CH-8001 Zürich
Tel: (41 1) 22 13-7 02; Fax: (41 1) 22 13-7 66

Turkey
Delegierter der Deutschen Wirtschaft
Representative of the German Economy
Muallim Naci Cad. 118/4 (P.K. 22),
TR-80840 Ortaköy-Istanbul
Tel: (90 1) 15 91-1 95; -1 96;
Fax: (90 1) 15 91-9 39

Taiwan
Deutsches Wirtschaftsbüro in Taipei
German Trade Office
4. Fl. 350, Min-Sheng E. Road, Taipei 10444
Tel: (88 62) 5 06-90 28; -24 67;
Fax: (88 62) 5 06-81 82

United Kingdom
Deutsche Industrie- und Handelskammer in
Großbritannien und Nordirland
German Chamber of Industry and Commerce
16 Buckingham Gate, London SW1E 6LB
Tel: (44 71) 2 33-56 56; Fax: (44 71) 2 33-78 35

USA
German-American Chambers of Commerce

New York
German-American Chamber of Commerce, Inc.
666 Fifth Avenue, New York, N.Y. 10103
Tel: (1 212) 9 74-88 39; Fax: (1 212) 9 74-88 67

Chicago
German-American Chamber of Commerce of
Chicago, Inc.
104 S. Michigan Ave., Suite 600,
Chicago, Ill. 60603-5978
Tel: (1 312) 7 82-85 57; Fax: (1 312) 7 82-38 92

Los Angeles
German-American Chamber of Commerce of
Los Angeles, Inc.
3250 Wilshire Blvd., Suite 1612,
Los Angeles, CA 90010
Tel: (1 213) 3 81-22 36; -2237;
Fax: (1 213) 3 81-34 49

San Francisco
German-American Chamber of Commerce of
San Francisco, Inc.
465 California Street, Suite 910; San Francisco,
CA 94104
Tel: (1 415) 3 92-22 62; Fax: (1 415) 3 92-13 14

Washington
Representative of German Industry and Trade
(Association of German Chambers of Industry
and Commerce
1 Farragut Square South, NW,
Washington, D.C. 20006
Tel: (1 202) 3 47-02 47; Fax: (1 202) 6 28-36 85

Associations of German Industry

Bundesverband der Deutschen Industrie e.V.
(BDI)
Federation of German Industries
Gustav-Heinemann-Ufer 84-88, W-5000 Köln 51
Tel: (0221) 37 08 00; Fax: (0221) 8 88 26 01
*The BDI is the umbrella organization of
30 trade organizations, the top organization of
the industrial trades.*

Bundesvereinigung der Deutschen Arbeitgeber-
verbände e.V. (BDA)
Confederation of German Employers' Associa-
tions
Gustav-Heinemann-Ufer 72, W-5000 Köln 51
Tel: (0221) 37 95-0; Fax: (0221) 37 95-2 35

Bundesverband mittelständische Wirtschaft
Unternehmerverband Deutschlands e.V.
Federal Association for Small and Medium-
sized Enterprises
Adenauerallee 13 b-c, W-5300 Bonn 1
Tel: (0228) 21 83 38; Fax: (0228) 22 16 91
*This organization features 32 member
associations and more than 10,000 members.
Representative for the new Länder is
Dr. Klaus Brandenburg
(Rodelbergweg 6, O-1195 Berlin;
Tel. and Fax: (0037-2-63 22 80 09)*

Institut für Mittelstandsforschung (IfM)
Small Business Research Institute
Maximilianstr. 20, W-5300 Bonn 1
Tel: (0228) 7 29 97-0; Fax: (0228) 7 29 97-34

Zentralverband des Deutschen Handwerks
(ZDH)
German Federation of Small Business and Crafts
Johanniterstr. 1, W-5300 Bonn
Tel: (0228) 5 45-0; Fax: (0228) 5 45-2 05

Bundesverband des Deutschen Groß- und
Außenhandels e.v. (BGA)
Federation of German Wholesale and Foreign
Trade
Kaiser-Friedrich-Str. 13, W-5300 Bonn
Tel: (0228) 2 60 04-0; Fax: (0228) 2 60 04-55

Hauptgemeinschaft des Deutschen
Einzelhandels e.v. (HDE)
Confederation of German Retailers
Sachsenring 89, W-5000 Köln 1
Tel: (0221) 33 98-0; Fax: (0221) 33 98-1 19

Bundesverband Deutscher Banken e.v.
Federation of the German Banking Industry
Mohrenstr. 35-41, W-5000 Köln 1
Tel: (0221) 16 63-0; Fax: (0221) 16 63-2 22

Gesamtverband der Deutschen Versicherungs-
wirtschaft e.v.
German Insurance Association
Walter-Flexstr. 3, W-5300 Bonn 1
Tel: (0228) 91 62-0; Fax: (0228) 91 62-2 00

Centralvereinigung Deutscher Handelsvertreter
und Handelsmakler-Verbände (CDH)
General Association of Commercial Agents and
Brokers
Geleniusstr. 1, W-5000 Köln 41
Tel: (0221) 51 40 43-44; Fax: (0221) 52 57 67

Ausstellungs- und Messe-Ausschuß der
Deutschen Wirtschaft e.v. (AUMA)
Confederation of German Trade Fair and
Exhibition Industries
Lindenstr. 8, W-5000 Köln 1
Tel: (0221) 2 09 07-0; Fax: (0221) 2 09 07-12

Vereinigung von Unternehmerinnen e.v.
Association of German Businesswomen
Gustav-Heinemann-Ufer 94, W-5000 Köln 51
Tel: (0221) 37 50 74-75; Fax: (0221) 34 31 71

Deutscher Franchise-Verband e.v. (DFV)
German Franchising Association
St.-Paul-Str. 9, W-8000 München 2
Tel: (089) 53 50 27; Fax: (089) 53 13 23

Ring Deutscher Makler Verband der
Immobilienberufe und Hausverwalter
Bundesverband e.v.
Umbrella organization for real estate
professions
Mönckebergstr. 27, W-2000 Hamburg 1
Tel: (040) 33 12 10, 33 12 19;
Fax: (040) 33 58 83

Arbeitsgemeinschaft der deutschen
Wertpapierbörsen
Federation of the German Stock Exchanges
Biebergasse 6-10, W-6000 Frankfurt a.M. 1
Tel: (069) 29 99 03-0; Fax: (069) 29 99 03-30

EC Liaison Offices in the New Länder

Dresden (affiliated with Deutsche Gesellschaft
für Mittelstandsforschung mbH)
Budapester Str. 5, O-8010 Dresden
Tel: (00 37 51) 4 85 22-46, -48; Fax: (00 37 51) 4
95 31 52
Representative: Karin Geweche

Erfurt (affiliated with Sparkassen und
Giroverband Ost)
Bezirksstelle Erfurt
Neuwerkstr. 3, O-5010 Erfurt
Tel: (00 37 61) 2 20 94

Frankfurt/Oder (affiliated with Chamber of
Industry and Commerce)
Postfach 343, Humboldtstr. 3,
O-1200 Frankfurt an der Oder
Tel: (00 37 30) 31 13 12; Fax: (00 37 30) 32 54 92
Representative: Britta Bayer

Leipzig (affiliated with Chamber of Industry
and Commerce)
Friedrich-Engels-Platz 5, O-7010 Leipzig
Tel: (00 37 41) 7 15 34 40;
Fax: (00 37 41) 7 15 34 21

Magdeburg (affiliated with Chamber of
Commerce)
Humboldtstr. 16, O-3014 Magdeburg
Tel: (00 37 91) 3 18-55, -59;
Fax: (00 37 91) 4 23 08

Rostock (affiliated with Chamber of Industry and Commerce)
Ernst-Barlach-Str. 7, O-2500 Rostock
Tel: (00 37 81) 3 75 01; Fax: (00 37 81) 2 29 19

Potsdam (affiliated with Wirtschaftsförderungs-GmbH)
Mangerstr. 35, O-1500 Potsdam
The office in Potsdam in process of being established, therefore no phone number yet

For more information on EC liaison offices in the new *Länder*, please contact:
Kommission der EG Vertretung in der Bundesrepublik Deutschland
Commission of the EC, Representation in Germany
Zitelmannstr. 22, W-5300 Bonn
Tel: (0228) 5 30 09-0; Fax: (0228) 5 30 09-50

Unions

Deutscher Gewerkschaftsbund (DGB) - Bundesvorstand
Federation of German Trade Unions - National Executive
Hans-Böckler-Str. 39, W-4000 Düsseldorf 30
Tel: (0211) 43 01-0; Fax: (0221) 43 01-3 24, -4 71
Umbrella organization embracing 16 unions

Deutsche Angestellten Gewerkschaft (DAG)
German Union of Salaried Employees
Karl-Muck-Platz 1, W-2000 Hamburg 36
Tel: (040) 3 49 15-1; Fax: (040) 3 49 15-4 00

Employers' Associations

See Bundesvereinigung der Deutschen Arbeitgeberverbände e.V. under
Associations of German Industry.

Selected Research Institutes

Deutsches Institut für Wirtschaftsforschung e.V. (DIW)
German Institute for Economic Research
Königin-Luise-Str. 5, W-1000 Berlin 33
Tel: (030) 8 29 91-0; Fax: (030) 8 29 91-2 00

Institut der deutschen Wirtschaft e.V. (IW)
G.-Heinemann-Ufer 84-88, W-5000 Köln 51
Tel: (0221) 37 08-01; Fax: (0221)37 08-192

Ifo-Institut für Wirschaftsforschung e.V.
Economic Research Institute
Poschingerstr. 5, W-8000 München 86
Tel: (089) 9 22 40; Fax: (089) 98 53 69

Ost-Ausschuß der Deutschen Wirtschaft
German East-West Trade Committee
Gustav-Heinemann-Ufer 84-88, W-5000 Köln 51
Tel: (0221) 37 08-4 17; Fax: (0221) 37 08-7 30
The trade committee helps setting up contacts between eastern and western business partners.

Bundesinstitut für ostwissenschaftliche und internationale Studien
Federal Institute for Eastern and International Studies
Lindenbornstr. 22, W-5000 Köln 30
Tel: (0221) 57 47-0; Fax: (0221) 57 47-1 10

Institut für Europäische Umweltpolitik
Institute for European Environmental Policy
Aloys-Schulte-Str. 6, W-5300 Bonn 1
Tel: (0228) 21 38 10; Fax: (0228) 22 19 82

Forschungsinstitut der Deutschen Gesellschaft für Auswärtige Politik e.V.
Research Institute of the German Council on Foreign Affairs
Adenauerallee 131, W-5300 Bonn 1
Tel: (0228) 26 75-0; Fax: (0228) 26 75-1 73

Akademie für Politische Bildung
Academy for Political Education
Buchensee 1, W-8132 Tutzing
Tel: (08158) 256-0; Fax: (08158) 256-14

Transportation and Leisure

Deutsche Bundesbahn
(German railway system in the old *Länder*)
Zentrale Hauptverwaltung (central
administration)
Friedrich-Ebert-Anlage 43-45,
W-6000 Frankfurt a.M. 1
Tel: (069) 2 65-1; Fax: (069) 2 65-64 80

Deutsche Reichsbahn
(German railway system in the new *Länder*)
Generaldirektion (central administration)
Ruschestr. 59, O-1130 Berlin
Tel: (0037-2) 23 72 23 09

Allgemeiner Deutscher Automobil-Club e.V.
(ADAC)
(main automobile club in Germany)
Am Westpark 8, W-8000 München 70
Tel: (089) 76 76-0; Fax: 76 76-25 00

Verband Deutscher Reeder e.V.
German Shipowners' Association
Esplanade 6, W-2000 Hamburg 36
Tel: (040) 3 50 97-0; Fax: (040) 3 50 97-2 11

Arbeitsgemeinschaft Deutscher Verkehrsflug-
häfen e.V. (ADV)
German Airports Association
Flughafen, W-7000 Stuttgart 23
Tel: (0711) 79 01-9 33, -9 34;
Fax: (0711) 79 01-7 46

Deutsche Lufthansa AG
Von-Gablenz-Str. 2-6, W-5000 Köln 21
Tel: (0221) 8 26-1; Fax: (0221) 8 26-38 18

Deutsche Zentrale für Tourismus e.V.
German National Tourist Board
Beethovenstr. 69, W-6000 Frankfurt a.M. 1
Tel: (069) 75 72-0; Fax: (069) 75 19 03

Deutscher Hotel- und Gaststättenverband e.V.
German Hotel and Restaurant Association
Kronprinzenstr. 46, W-5300 Bonn 2
Tel: (0228) 8 20 08-0; Fax: (0228) 8 20 08-46

Embassies

Australia
Godesberger Allee 105-107, W-5300 Bonn 2
Tel: (0228) 81 03-0; Fax: (0228) 37 62 68

Austria
Johanniterstr. 2, W-5300 Bonn 1
Tel: (0228) 5 30 06-0; Fax: (0228) 5 30 06-45

Belgium
Kaiser-Friedrich-Str. 7, W-5300 Bonn 1
Tel: (0228) 21 20 01-05, Fax: (0228) 22 08 57

Canada
Friedrich-Wilhelm-Str. 18, W-5300 Bonn 1
Tel: (0228) 23 10 61; Fax: (0228) 23 08 57

Czechoslovakia
Ferdinandstr. 27, W-5300 Bonn 1
Tel: (0228) 28 52 87, 28 52 92, 28 50 81, 28 25
80;
Fax: (0228) 28 43 69

Denmark
Pfälzer Str. 14, P.O. Box 18 02 20,
W-5300 Bonn 1
Tel: (0228) 7 29 91-0; Fax: (0228) 7 29 91-31

Egypt
Kronprinzenstr. 2, W-5300 Bonn 2
Tel: (0228) 36 40-00,-08,-09;
Fax: (0228) 36 43 04

Finland
Friesdorfer Str. 1, W-5300 Bonn 2
Tel: (0228) 31 82 98-0; Fax: (0228) 3 82 98-50

France
Kapellenweg 1a, W-5300 Bonn 2
Tel: (0228) 36 20 31-36; Fax: (0228) 35 18 32

Greece
Koblenzer Str. 103, W-5300 Bonn 2
Tel: (0228) 83 01-0; Fax: (0228) 35 32 84

India
Adenauerallee 262-264, W-5300 Bonn 1
Tel: (0228) 54 05-0; Fax: (0228) 54 05-1 53, -154

Israel
Simrockallee 2, W-5300 Bonn 2
Tel: (0228) 82 31-0; Fax: (0228) 35 60 93

Italy
Karl-Finkelnburg-Str. 51, W-5300 Bonn 2
Tel: (0228) 8 20 06-0; Fax: (0228) 8 20 06 69

Japan
Bonn-Center HI-701, Bundeskanzlerplatz,
W-5300 Bonn 1
Tel: (0228) 8191-0; Fax: (0228) 37 93 99

Jugoslavia
Schloßallee 5, W-5300 Bonn 2
Tel: (0228) 34 40 51-56, Fax: (0228) 34 40 57

Kuwait
Godesberger Allee 77-81, W-5300 Bonn 2
Tel: (0228) 37 80 81-83; Fax: (0228) 37 61 82

Netherlands
Sträßchensweg 10, W-5300 Bonn 1
Tel: (0228) 53 05-0; Fax: (0228) 23 86 21

New Zealand
Bonn-Center, HI 902, Bundeskanzlerplatz 2-10,
W-5300 Bonn 1
Tel: (0228) 2 28 97-0; Fax: (0228) 22 16 87

Norway
Mittelstr. 43, W-5300 Bonn 2
Tel: (0228) 81 99 70; Fax: (0228) 37 34 98

People's Republic of China
Kurfürstenallee 12, W-5300 Bonn 2
Tel: (0228) 36 10 95-98, 36 38 26;
Fax: (0228) 36 16 35

Poland
Lindenallee 7, W-5000 Köln 51
Tel: (0221) 38 02 61-65; Fax: (0221) 34 30 89

Portugal
Ubierstr. 78, W-5300 Bonn 2
Tel: (0228) 36 30 11-16; Fax: (0228) 35 28 64

Saudi Arabia
Godesberger Allee 40-42, W-5300 Bonn 2
Tel: (0228) 37 90 13-17, 37 80 18-19;
Fax: (0228) 37 55 93

South Korea
Adenauerallee 124, W-5300 Bonn 1
Tel: (0228) 26 79 60; Fax: (0228) 22 39 43

Soviet Union
Waldstr. 42, P.O. Box 20 09 08, W-5300 Bonn 2
Tel: (0228) 31 20-74, -86, -87, -92;
Fax: (0228) 38 45 61

Spain
Schloßstr. 4, W-5300 Bonn 1
Tel: (0228) 21 70 94-95; Fax: (0228) 22 34 05

Sweden
Heussallee 2-10, W-5300 Bonn 1
Tel: (0228) 2 60 02-0; Fax: (0228) 22 38 37

Switzerland
Gotenstr. 156, W-5300 Bonn 2
Tel: (0228) 81 00 80; Fax: (0228) 8 10 08 19

Taiwan
(no embassy)
Taipei Wirtschafts- und Kulturbüro
Taipei Economic and Cultural Office
Villichgasse 17/IV, W-5300 Bonn 2
Tel: (0228) 36 40 14-18; Fax: (0228) 35 48 74

Turkey
Utestr. 47, W-5300 Bonn 2
Tel: (0228) 34 60 52-54; Fax: (0228)34 88 77

United Kingdom
Friedrich-Ebert-Allee 77, W-5300 Bonn 1
Tel: (0228) 23 40 61;
Fax: (0228) 23 40 70, 23 70 58

USA
Deichmanns Aue 29, P.O. Box 240,
W-5300 Bonn 2
Tel: (0228) 3 39-1; Fax: (0228) 3 39-26 63

Other

European Initiative for Eastern Germany
Postfach 10 05 05, W-6000 Frankfurt/Main 1
Tel: (069) 13 62-26 36; Fax: (069) 13 62-20 08

Deutscher Franchise-Verband (DFV)
(German Franchising Association)
St.-Paul-Str. 9, W-8000 München 2
Tel: (089) 53 50 27; Fax: (089) 53 13 231

Goethe-Institut
Lenbachplatz 3, W-8000 München 2
Tel: (089) 41 86 80; Fax: (089) 41 86 84 14
The Goethe Institute furthers German language and culture in foreign countries.

Deutsches Rotes Kreuz e.V. (DRK)
German Red Cross
Friedrich-Ebert-Allee 71, W-5300 Bonn 1
Tel: (0228) 5 41-1; Fax: (0228) 5 41-2 90

Arbeitsgemeinschaft der Verbraucherverbände e.V.
Organization of Consumers' Associations
Heilsbacherstr. 20, W-5300 Bonn 1
Tel: (0228) 64 89-0; Fax: (0228) 64 42 58

C Miscellaneous

School Holidays

Land	Autumn 1991	Christmas 1991/92	Winter 1992	Easter 1992	Whitsun 1992
Baden-Württ.	25 - 30 Oct.	23 Dec. - 4 Jan.	2 - 6 March	13 - 25 April	1 - 5 June
Bayern	28 Oct. - 2 Nov.	23 Dec. - 4 Jan.	–	13 - 25 April	9 - 20 June
Berlin[1]	26 Oct. - 2 Nov.	23 Dec. - 6 Jan.	–	4 - 25 April	6 - 9 June
Brandenburg[1]	21 - 25 Oct.	23 Dec. - 3 Jan.	10 - 21 Febr.	14 - 16 April	5 - 9 June
Bremen	14 - 19 Oct.	23 Dec. - 6 Jan.	–	1 - 21 April	–
Hamburg	7 - 19 Oct.	23 Dec. - 4 Jan.	9 - 21 March[2]	16 - 21 April	29 May
Hessen	7 - 18 Oct.	23 Dec. - 11 Jan.	–	3 - 22 April	–
Mecklenburg-Vorpommern[1]	21 - 25 Oct.	23 Dec. - 3 Jan.	17 - 28 Febr.	15 - 21 April	5 - 9 June
Niedersachsen	10 - 19 Oct.	21 Dec. - 6 Jan.	–	1 - 21 April	6 - 9 June
Nordrhein-Westfalen	21 - 26 Oct.	23 Dec. - 6 Jan.	–	6 - 25 April	9 June
Rheinland-Pfalz	21 - 26 Oct.	23 Dec. - 8 Jan.	–	6 - 25 April	9 June
Saarland	7 - 19 Oct.	23 Dec. - 6 Jan.	2 - 3 March[3]	13 - 27 April	–
Sachsen[1]	14 - 18 Oct.	23 Dec. - 3 Jan.	20 - 28 Febr.	16 - 24 April	4 - 9 June
Sachsen-Anhalt[1]	21 - 25 Oct.	23 Dec. - 6 Jan.	17 - 21 Febr.	13 - 21 April	4 - 10 June
Schleswig-Holstein	14 - 26 Oct.	23 Dec. - 6 Jan.	–	9 - 25 April	–
Thüringen[1]	21 - 25 Oct.	23 Dec. - 3 Jan.	10 - 21 Febr.	13 - 16 April	5 - 9 June

1 Complete holidays for this *Land* are not yet available.
2 Spring Holidays
3 Carnival

Summer 1992	Autumn 1992	Christmas 1992/93	Winter 1993	Easter 1993	Whitsun 1993
2 July - 15 Aug.	26 - 30 Oct.	23 Dec. - 5 Jan.			
30 July - 14 Sept.	–	23 Dec. - 9 Jan.	–	5 - 17 April	1 - 12 June
25 June - 8 Aug.	2 - 10 Oct.	23 Dec. - 6 Jan.	–		
29 June - 7 Aug.					
25 June - 8 Aug.	5 - 13 Oct.	23 Dec. - 6 Jan.	–	29 Mar. - 17 Apr.	–
18 June - 1 Aug.	5 - 17 Oct.	21 Dec. - 2 Jan.	–	8 - 20 March	17 - 22 May
22 June - 31 July	5 - 16 Oct.	23 Dec. - 8 Jan.	–	5 - 23 April	–
13 July - 21 Aug.	–				
25 June - 5 Aug.	28 Sept. - 10 Oct.	23 Dec. - 6 Jan.	–	27 Mar. - 17 Apr.	29 May - 1 June
16 July - 29 Aug.	19 - 24 Oct.	23 Dec. - 6 Jan.	–	29 Mar. - 17 Apr.	1 June
23 July - 2 Sept.	19 - 24 Oct.	23 Dec. - 9 Jan.	–	29 Mar. - 16 Apr.	1 June
23 July - 5 Sept.	26 - 31 Oct.	21 Dec. - 6 Jan.	22 - 23 Febr.[3]	1 - 19 April	–
6 July - 14 Aug.	–				
20 July - 28 Aug.	–				
18 June - 1 Aug.	5 - 17 Oct.	23 Dec. - 7 Jan.	–	5 - 17 April	–
13 July - 21 Aug.	–				

Legal Holidays

1991	1992	German	English
Jan. 1	Jan. 1	Neujahr	New Year's Day
Jan. 6	Jan. 6	Heilige Drei Könige	Epiphany[1]
March 29	April 17	Karfreitag	Good Friday
March 31	April 19	Ostersonntag	Easter Sunday
April 1	April 20	Ostermontag	Easter Monday
May 1	May 1	Tag der Arbeit	Labour Day
May 9	May 28	Christi Himmelfahrt	Ascension
May 19	June 7	Pfingstsonntag	Whit Sunday
May 20	June 8	Pfingstmontag	Whit Monday
May 30	June 18	Fronleichnam	Corpus Christi[2]
Aug. 15	Aug. 15	Mariä Himmelfahrt	Assumption (of the Blessed Virgin)[3]
Oct. 3	Oct. 3	Tag der Deutschen Einheit	German Unity Day
Oct. 31	Oct. 31	Reformationstag	Reformation Day[4]
Nov. 1	Nov. 1	Allerheiligen	All Saints' Day[5]
Nov. 20	Nov. 18	Buß- und Bettag	Day of Repentance and Prayer
Dec. 25	Dec. 25	1. Weihnachtstag	Christmas Day
Dec. 26	Dec. 26	2. Weihnachtstag	Boxing Day

1 Baden-Württemberg and Bayern
2 Baden Württemberg, Bayern, Hessen, Nordrhein-Westfalen, Rheinland-Pfalz, Saarland
3 Parts of Bayern, Saarland
4 Brandenburg, Mecklenburg-Vorpommern, Sachsen, Sachsen-Anhalt, Thüringen
5 Baden-Württemberg, Bayern, Nordrhein-Westfalen, Rheinland-Pfalz, Saarland, parts of Thüringen

Phoning within Germany

It used to be that phoning from former West Germany to former East Germany or vice versa was virtually impossible. In November 1989 only 690 phone lines existed from West to East and only 111 from East to West. The current "phone situation" is no longer quite as bad, and the former western and former eastern telecommunications companies which fused after unificiation have set the ambitious goal of installing over 7 million phone connections by 1997.

Since 6 July 1990, phoning between the eastern and western part of Germany has been eased by an additional 22,000 phone connections bringing the June 1991 total up to 30,000.

By the end of 1991, extended mobile-phone connections in conurbations and along *Autobahns* will make it possible to use mobile phones throughout the eastern *Länder*. (Currently, mobile-phoning can be difficult in rural areas or where too many mobile phones are being used.)

The Treuhand head office and the Berlin offices of federal ministries which are situated in the eastern part of Berlin have privileged "western" phone lines.

Shopping in Germany

There must be some Murphy-type law that says that the more inconvenient it is to do something, the more popular that activity becomes. Such a law or principle would seem to apply in the case of shopping in Germany. Shopping hours are strictly regulated throughout the country and as a result, shops are rarely open when one needs them (after work or during most of the weekend, for example). Nevertheless, Germans are avid shoppers and retailers are obviously happy enough with their turnover that they see little reason to lobby for more convenient (for the customer) or longer opening hours. On the contrary; most retailers and their unions are dead against another open minute and have vehemently opposed any move to keep shops open after 6:30 p.m. on weekdays, and after 2 p.m. on Saturdays (except on the first Saturday of every month, and all of the Saturdays in December, where shops may remain open until 6 p.m.). Sunday is an absolute no-no. Fierce battles fought over many years finally ended with a compromise: shops may now stay open until 8:30 p.m. on Thursdays – but must close at 4 p.m. on the six "long" Saturdays in the summer. Note the "may" throughout the above: shops do not have to stay open for as long as they may, and many (outside city centres) do not. In fact, they often open late (around 9 p.m., boutiques even later), close early (around 6 p.m.), take a couple of hours off for lunch (either between midday and 2 p.m., or between 1 p.m. and 3 p.m.) and ignore late Thursdays and long Saturdays. The visitor to Germany is not encouraged to spend his money in German shops, but rather, to buy German at home (where presumably he can find open shops more easily).